W9-DEC-378

The Politics
of Truth

Michel Foucault

Edited by Sylvère Lotringer & Lysa Hochroth

Semiotext(e)

Copyright @1997 Semiotext(e)

Special thanks to Mark Blasius, Jessica Blatt
and the New Press, Sande Cohen,
Peter Gente, Mary Kelly, Heidi Paris,
Paul Rabinow, & Dominique Seglard

Semiotext(e) Offices

522 Philosophy Hall
Columbia University
New York, New York
10027

POB 568
Williamsburgh Station
Brooklyn, New York
11211-0568

Phone & Fax: 718-963-2603

Printed in the United States of America

Contents

Was ist Aufklärung?
Immanuel Kant

Enlightenment is man's release from his self-incurred tutelage. Tutelage is man's inability to make use of his understanding without direction from another. Self-incurred is this tutelage when its cause lies not in lack of reason but in lack of resolution and courage to use it without direction from another. *Sapere aude!*[1] "Have courage to use your own reason!"—that is the motto of enlightenment.

Laziness and cowardice are the reasons why so great a portion of mankind, after nature has long since discharged them from external direction (*naturaliter maiorennes*), nevertheless remains under lifelong tutelage, and why it is so easy for others to set themselves up as their guardians. It is so easy not to be of age. If I have a book which understancds for me, a pastor who has a conscience for me, a physician who decides my diet,

7

and so forth, I need not trouble myself. I need not think, if I can only pay—others will readily undertake the irksome work for me.

That the step to competence is held to be very dangerous by the far greater portion of mankind (and by the entire fair sex)—quite apart from its being arduous—is seen to by those guardians who have so kindly assumed superintendence over them. After the guardians have first made their domestic cattle dumb and have made sure that these placid creatures will not dare take a single step without the harness of the cart to which they are tethered, the guardians then show them the danger which threatens if they try to go alone. Actually, however, this danger is not so great, for by falling a few times they would finally learn to walk alone. But an example of this failure makes them timid and ordinarily frightens them away from all further trials.

For any single individual to work himself out of the life under tutelage which has become almost his nature is very difficult. He has come to be fond of this state, and he is for the present really incapable of making use of his reason, for no one has ever let him try it out. Statutes and formulas, those mechanical tools of the rational employment or rather misemployment of his natural gifts, are the

The Politics of Truth

Michel Foucault

SEMIOTEXT(E) FOREIGN AGENTS SERIES
Jim Fleming & Sylvère Lotringer, Editors

fetters of an everlasting tutelage. Whoever throws them off makes only an uncertain leap over the narrowest ditch because he is not accustomed to that kind of free motion. Therefore, there are few who have succeeded by their own exercise of mind both in freeing themselves from incompetence and in achieving a steady pace.

But that the public should enlighten itself is more possible; indeed, if only freedom is granted, enlightenment is almost sure to follow. For there will always be some independent thinkers, even among the established guardians of the great masses, who, after throwing off the yoke of tutelage from their own shoulders, will disseminate the spirit of the rational appreciation of both their own worth and every man's vocation for thinking for himself. But be it noted that the public, which has first been brought under this yoke by their guardians, forces the guardians themselves to remain bound when it is incited to do so by some of the guardians who are themselves capable of some enlightenment — so harmful is it to implant prejudices, for they later take vengeance on their cultivators or on their descendants. Thus the public can only slowly attain enlightenment. Perhaps a fall of personal despotism or of avaricious or tyrannical oppression may be accomplished by revolution, but never a true reform in ways of thinking. Rather, new prejudices will serve as well as old ones to harness the great unthinking masses.

For this enlightenment, however, nothing is required but freedom, and indeed the most harmless among all the things to which this term can properly be applied. It is the freedom to make public use of one's reason at every point.[2] But I hear on all sides, "Do not argue!" The officer says: "Do not argue but drill!" The tax collector: "Do not argue but pay!" The cleric: "Do not argue but believe!" Only one prince in the world says, "Argue as much as you will, and about what you will, but obey!" Everywhere there is restriction on freedom.

Which restriction is an obstacle to enlightenment, and which is not an obstacle but a promoter of it? I answer: The public use of one's reason must always be free, and it alone can bring about enlightenment among men. The private use of reason, on the other hand, may often be very narrowly restricted without particularly hindering the progress of enlightenment. By the public use of one's reason I understand the use which a person makes of it as a scholar before the reading public. Private use I call that which one may make of it in a particular civil post or office which is entrusted to him. Many affairs which are conducted in the interest of the community require a certain mechanism through which some members of the community must passively conduct themselves with an artificial unanimity, so that the government may direct them to public ends, or at least prevent them from destroying those ends. Here argument is certainly not allowed — one must obey. But so far as a part of the mechanism regards himself at the same time as a member of the whole community or of a society of world citizens, and thus in the role of a scholar who addresses the public (in the proper sense of the word) through his writings, he certainly can argue without hurting the affairs for which he is in part responsible as a passive member. Thus it would be ruinous for an officer in service to debate about the suitability or utility of a command given to him by his superior; he must obey. But the right to make remarks on errors in the military service and to lay them before the public for judgment cannot equitably be refused him as a scholar. The citizen cannot refuse to pay the taxes imposed on him; indeed, an impudent complaint at those levied on him can be punished as a scandal (as it could occasion general refractoriness). But the same person nevertheless does not act contrary to his duty as a citizen when, as a scholar, he publicly expresses his thoughts on the

inappropriateness or even the injustice of these
levies. Similarly a clergyman is obligated to make
his sermon to his pupils in catechism and his congregation conform to the symbol of the church
which he serves, for he has been accepted on this
condition. But as a scholar he has complete freedom, even the calling, to communicate to the public all his carefully tested and well-meaning
thoughts on that which is erroneous in the symbol
and to make suggestions for the better organization of the religious body and church. In doing this
there is nothing that could be laid as a burden on
his conscience. For what he teaches as a consequence of his office as a representative of the
church, this he considers something about which
he has no freedom to teach according to his own
lights; it is something which he is appointed to pro-
pound at the dictation of and in the name of another. He will say, "Our church teaches this or that;
those are the proofs which it adduces." He thus
extracts all practical uses for his congregation from
statutes to which he himself would not subscribe
with full conviction but to the enunciation of
which he can very well pledge himself because it is
not impossible that truth lies hidden in them, and,
in any case, there is at least nothing in them con-
tradictory to inner religion. For if he believed he

had found such in them, he could not conscientiously discharge the duties of his office; he would have to give it up. The use, therefore, which an appointed teacher makes of his reason before his congregation is merely private, because this congregation is only a domestic one (even if it be a large gathering); with respect to it, as a priest, he is not free, nor can he be free, because he carries out the orders of another. But as a scholar, whose writings speak to his public, the world, the clergyman in the public use of his reason enjoys an unlimited freedom to use his own reason and to speak in his own person. That the guardians of the people (in spiritual things) should themselves be incompetent is an absurdity which amounts to the eternalization of absurdities.

But would not a society of clergymen, perhaps a church conference or a venerable classis (as they call themselves among the Dutch), be justified in obligating itself by oath to a certain unchangeable symbol in order to enjoy an unceasing guardianship over each of its members and thereby over the people as a whole, and even to make it eternal? I answer that this is altogether impossible. Such a contract, made to shut off all further enlightenment from the human race, is absolutely null and void even if confirmed by the supreme power, by parliaments, and by the most ceremonious of peace treaties. An age cannot bind itself and ordain to put the succeeding one into such a condition that it cannot extend its (at best very occasional) knowledge, purify itself of errors, and progress in general enlightenment. That would be a crime against human nature, the proper destination of which lies precisely in this progress; and the descendants would be fully justified in rejecting those decrees as having been made in an unwarranted and malicious manner.

The touchstone of everything that can be concluded as a law for a people lies in the question whether the people could have imposed such a law on itself. Now such a religious compact might be possible for a short and definitely limited time, as it were, in expectation of a better. One might let every citizen, and especially the clergyman, in the role of scholar, make his comments freely and publicly, i.e., through writing, on the erroneous aspects of the present institution. The newly introduced order might last until insight into the nature of these things had become so general and widely approved that through uniting their voices (even if not unanimously) they could bring a proposal to the throne to take those congregations under protection which had united into a changed religious

organization according to their better ideas, without, however, hindering others who wish to remain
in the order. But to unite in a permanent religious
institution which is not to be subject to doubt
before the public even in the lifetime of one man,
and thereby to make a period of time fruitless in
the progress of mankind toward improvement,
thus working to the disadvantage of posterity—
that is absolutely forbidden. For himself (and only
for a short time) a man may postpone enlightenment in what he ought to know, but to renounce it
for himself and even more to renounce it for posterity is to injure and trample on the rights of
mankind.

And what a people may not decree for itself
can even less be decreed for them by a monarch,
for his lawgiving authority rests on his uniting the
general public will in his own. If he only sees to it
that all true or alleged improvement stands together with civil order, he can leave it to his subjects to
do what they find necessary for their spiritual welfare. This is not his concern, though it is incum-
bent on him to prevent one of them from violently
hindering another in determining and promoting
this welfare to the best of his ability. To meddle in
these matters lowers his own majesty, since by the
writings in which his subjects seek to present their

views he may evaluate his own governance. He can do this when, with deepest understanding, he lays upon himself the reproach, *Caesar non est supra grammaticos.* Far more does he injure his own majesty when he degrades his supreme power by supporting the ecclesiastical despotism of some tyrants in his state over his other subjects.

If we are asked, "Do we now live in an *enlightened age*?" the answer is, "No," but we do live in an *age of enlightenment.*[3] As things now stand, much is lacking which prevents men from being, or easily becoming, capable of correctly using their own reason in religious matters with assurance and free from outside direction. But, on the other hand, we have clear indications that the field has now been opened wherein men may freely deal with these things and that the obstacles to general enlightenment or the release from self-imposed tutelage are gradually being reduced. In this respect, this is the age of enlightenment, or the century of Frederick.

A prince who does not find it unworthy of himself to say that he holds it to be his duty to prescribe nothing to men in religious matters but to give them complete freedom while renouncing the haughty name of *tolerance,* is himself enlightened and deserves to be esteemed by the grateful world and posterity as the first, at least from the side of government, who divested the human race of its tutelage and left each man free to make use of his reason in matters of conscience. Under him venerable ecclesiastics are allowed, in the role of scholars, and without infringing on their official duties, freely to submit for public testing their judgments and views which here and there diverge from the established symbol. And an even greater freedom is enjoyed by those who are restricted by no official duties. This spirit of freedom spreads beyond this land, even to those in which it must struggle with external obstacles erected by a government which misunderstands its own interest. For an example gives evidence to such a government that in freedom there is not the least cause for concern about public peace and the stability of the community. Men work themselves gradually out of barbarity if only intentional artifices are not made to hold them in it.

I have placed the main point of enlightenment—the escape of men from their self-incurred tutelage—chiefly in matters of religion because our rulers have no interest in playing the guardian with respect to the arts and sciences and also because religious incompetence is not only the most harmful but also the most degrading of all. But the manner of thinking of the head of a state who favors religious enlightenment goes further, and he sees that there is no danger to his lawgiving in allowing his subjects to make public use of their reason and to publish their thoughts on a better formulation of his legislation and even their open-minded criticisms of the laws already made. Of this we have a shining example wherein no monarch is superior to him whom we honor

But only one who is himself enlightened, is not afraid of shadows, and has a numerous and well-disciplined army to assure public peace, can say: "Argue as much as you will, and about what you will, only obey!" A republic could not dare say such a thing. Here is shown a strange and unexpected trend in human affairs in which almost everything, looked at in the large, is paradoxical. A greater degree of civil freedom appears advantageous to the freedom of mind of the people, and yet it places inescapable limitations upon it; a lower degree of civil freedom, on the contrary, provides the mind with room for each man to extend himself to his full capacity. As nature has uncovered from under this hard shell the seed for which she most tenderly cares—the propensity and vocation to free thinking—this gradually works back upon the character of the people, who thereby gradually become capable of managing freedom; finally, it affects the principles of government, which finds it to its advantage to treat men, who are now more than machines, in accordance with their dignity.[4]

Königsberg, Prussia
September 30, 1784

1 ["Dare to know!" (Horace, *Ars poetica*). This was the motto adopted in 1736 by the Society of the Friends of Truth, an important circle in the German Enlightenment. Tr.]

2 [It is this freedom Kant claimed later in his conflict with the censor, deferring to the censor in the "private" use of reason, i.e., in his lectures. Tr.]

3 ["Our age is, in especial degree, the age of criticism, and to criticism everything must submit." (*Critique of Pure Reason*, Preface to first ed., Smith trans.) Tr.]

4 Today I read in the *Büschingsche Wöchentliche Nachrichten* for September 13 an announcement of the *Berlinische Monatsschrift* for this month, which cites the answer to the same question by Herr Mendelssohn.* But this issue has not yet come to me; if it had, I would have held back the present essay, which is now put forth only

in order to see how much agreement in thought
can be brought about by chance.

*[Mendelssohn's answer was that enlighten-
   ment lay in intellectual cultivation, which
   he distinguished from the practical. Kant,
   quite in line with his later essay on theory
   and practice, refuses to make this distinction fundamental. Tr.]

I
CRITIQUE AND ENLIGHTENMENT

1
What is Critique?

HENRI GOUHIER[1]: Ladies and Gentlemen, I would first like to thank Mr. Michel Foucault for having made time in his busy schedule this year for this session, especially since we are catching him, not the day after, but only about two days after his long trip to Japan. This explains why the invitation for this meeting was rather terse. Since Michel Foucault's paper is in fact a surprise and, as we can assume, a good surprise, I will not have you wait any longer for the pleasure to hear it.

MICHEL FOUCAULT: I thank you very much for having invited me to this meeting before this Society. I believe that about ten years ago I gave a talk here on the subject entitled *What is an author?*[2]

For the issue about which I would like to speak today, I have no title. Mr. Gouhier has been indulgent enough to say that the reason for this was my trip to Japan. Truthfully, this is a very kind attenuation of the truth. Let's say, in fact, that up until a few days ago, I had hardly been able to find a title; or rather there was one that kept haunting me but that I didn't want to choose. You are going to see why: it would have been indecent.

Actually, the question about which I wanted to speak and about which I still want to speak is: *What is critique?* It might be worth trying out a few ideas on this project that keeps taking shape, being extended and reborn on the outer limits of philosophy, very close to it, up against it, at its expense, in the direction of a future philosophy and in lieu, perhaps, of all possible philosophy. And it seems that between the high Kantian enterprise and the little polemical professional activities that are called critique, it seems to me that there has been in the modern Western world (dating, more or less, empirically from the 15th to the 16th centuries) a certain way of thinking, speaking and acting, a certain relationship to what exists, to what one knows, to what one does, a relationship to society, to culture and also a relationship to others that we could call, let's say, the critical attitude. Of course, you will be surprised to hear that there is something like a critical attitude that would be specific to modern civilization, since there have been so many critiques, polemics, etc. and since even Kant's problems presumably have origins which go back way before the 15th and 16th centuries. One will be surprised to see that one tries to find a unity in this critique, although by its very nature, by its function, I was going to say, by its profession, it seems to be condemned to dispersion, dependency and pure heteronomy. After all, critique only exists in relation to something other than itself: it is an instrument, a means for a future or a truth that it will not know nor happen to be, it oversees a domain it would want to police and is unable to regulate. All this means that it is a function which is subordinated in relation to what philosophy, science, politics, ethics, law, literature, etc., positively constitute. And at the same time, whatever the pleasures or compensations accompanying this curious activity of critique, it seems that it rather regularly, almost always, brings not only some stiff bit of utility it claims to have, but also that it is supported by some kind of more general imperative — more general still than that of eradicating errors. There is something in critique which is akin to virtue. And in a certain way, what I wanted to speak to you about is this critical attitude as virtue in general.

There are several routes one could take to discuss the history of this critical attitude. I would simply like to suggest this one to you, which is one possible route, again, among many others. I will suggest the following variation: the Christian pastoral, or the Christian church inasmuch as it acted in a precisely and specifically pastoral way, developed this idea — singular and, I believe, quite foreign to ancient culture — that each individual, whatever his age or status, from the beginning to the end of his life and in his every action, had to be governed and had to let himself be governed, that is to say directed towards his salvation, by someone to whom he was bound by a total, meticulous, detailed relationship of obedience. And this salvation-oriented operation in a relationship of obedience to someone, has to be made in a triple relationship to the truth: truth understood as dogma, truth also to the degree where this orientation implies a special and individualizing knowledge of individuals; and finally, in that this direction is deployed like a reflective technique comprising general rules, particular knowledge, precepts, methods of examination, confessions, interviews, etc. After all, we must not forget what, for centuries, the Greek church called *technè technôn* and what the Latin Roman church called *ars artium*. It was precisely the direction of conscience; the art of governing men. Of course, this art of governing for a long time was linked to relatively limited practices, even in medieval society, to monastic life and especially to the practice of relatively restricted spiritual groups. But I believe that from the 15th century on and before the Reformation, one can say that there was a veritable explosion of the art of governing men. There was an explosion in two ways: first, by displacement in relation to the religious center, let's say if you will, secularization, the expansion in civil society of this theme of the art of governing men and the methods of doing it; and then, second, the proliferation of this art of governing into a variety of areas — how to govern children, how to govern the poor and beggars, how to govern a family, a house, how to govern armies, different groups, cities, States and also how to govern one's own body and mind. *How to govern* was, I believe, one of the fundamental questions about what was happening in the 15th or 16th centuries. It is a fundamental question which was answered by the multiplication of all the arts of governing — the art of pedagogy, the art of politics, the art of economics, if you will — and of all the institutions of government, in the wider sense the term government had at the time.

So, this governmentalization, which seems to me to be rather characteristic of these societies in Western Europe in the 16th century, cannot apparently be dissociated from the question "how not to be governed?" I do not mean by that that governmentalization would be opposed in a kind of face-off by the opposite affirmation, "we do not want to be governed, and we do not want to be governed *at all*." I mean that, in this great preoccupation about the way to govern and the search for the ways to govern, we identify a perpetual question which would be: "how not to be governed *like that*, by that, in the name of those principles, with such and such an objective in mind and by means of such procedures, not like that, not for that, not by them." And if we accord this movement of governmentalization of both society and individuals the historic dimension and breadth which I believe it has had, it seems that one could approximately locate therein what we could call the critical attitude. Facing them head on and as compensation, or rather, as both partner and adversary to the arts of governing, as an act of defiance, as a challenge, as a way of limiting these arts of governing and sizing them up, transforming them, of finding a way to escape from them or, in any case, a way to displace them, with a basic distrust, but also and by the same token, as a line of development of the arts of governing, there would have been something born in Europe at that time, a kind of general cultural form, both a political and moral attitude, a way of thinking, etc. and which I would very simply call the art of not being governed or better, the art of not being governed like that and at that cost. I would therefore propose, as a very first definition of critique, this general characterization: the art of not being governed quite so much.

You will tell me that this definition is both very general and very vague or fluid. Well, of course it is! But I still believe that it may allow us to identify some precise points inherent to what I try to call the critical attitude. These are historical anchoring points, of course, which we can determine as follows:

1. First anchoring point: during a period of time when governing men was essentially a spiritual art, or an essentially religious practice linked to the authority of a Church, to the prescription of a Scripture, not to want to be governed like that essentially meant finding another function for the Scriptures unrelated to the teaching of God. Not wanting to be governed was a certain way of refusing, challenging, limiting (say it as you like) eccle-

siastical rule. It meant returning to the Scriptures, seeking out what was authentic in them, what was really written in the Scriptures. It meant questioning what sort of truth the Scriptures told, gaining access to this truth of the Scriptures in the Scriptures and maybe in spite of what was written, to the point of finally raising the very simple question: were the Scriptures true? And, in short, from Wycliffe to Pierre Bayle, critique developed in part, for the most part, but not exclusively, of course, in relation to the Scriptures. Let us say that critique is biblical, historically.

2. Not to want to be governed, this is the second anchoring point. Not to want to be governed like that also means not wanting to accept these laws because they are unjust because, by virtue of their antiquity or the more or less threatening ascendancy given them by today's sovereign, they hide a fundamental illegitimacy. Therefore, from this perspective, confronted with government and the obedience it stipulates, critique means putting forth universal and indefeasible rights to which every government, whatever it may be, whether a monarch, a magistrate, an educator or a pater familias, will have to submit. In brief, if you like, we find here again the problem of natural law.

Natural law is certainly not an invention of the Renaissance, but from the 16th century on, it took on a critical function that it still maintains to this day. To the question "how not to be governed?" it answers by saying: "What are the limits of the right to govern?" Let us say that here critique is basically a legal issue.

3. And finally "to not to want to be governed" is of course not accepting as true, here I will move along quickly, what an authority tells you is true, or at least not accepting it because an authority tells you that it is true, but rather accepting it only if one considers valid the reasons for doing so. And this time, critique finds its anchoring point in the problem of certainty in its confrontation with authority.

The Bible, jurisprudence, science, writing, nature, the relationship to oneself; the sovereign, the law, the authority of dogmatism. One sees how the interplay of governmentalization and critique has brought about phenomena which are, I believe, of capital importance in the history of Western culture whether in the development of philological sciences, philosophical thought, legal analysis or methodological reflections. However, above all, one sees that the core of critique is basically made of the bundle of relationships that are tied to one another, or one to the two others, power, truth and the subject. And if governmentalization is indeed this movement through which individuals are subjugated in the reality of a social practice through mechanisms of power that adhere to a truth, well, then! I will say that critique is the movement by which the subject gives himself the right to question truth on its effects of power and question power on its discourses of truth. Well, then!: critique will be the art of voluntary insubordination, that of reflected intractability. Critique would essentially insure the desubjugation of the subject in the context of what we could call, in a word, the politics of truth.

I would have the arrogance to think that this definition, however empirical, approximate and deliciously distant its character in relation to the history it encompasses, is not very different from the one Kant provided: not to define critique, but precisely to define something else. It is not very far off in fact from the definition he was giving of the *Aufklärung*. It is indeed characteristic that, in his text from 1784, *What is the Aufklärung?*, he defined the *Aufklärung* in relation to a certain minority condition in which humanity was maintained and maintained in an authoritative way. Second, he defined this minority as characterized by a certain incapacity in which humanity was maintained, an incapacity to use its own understanding precisely without something which would be someone else's direction, and he uses *leiten*, which has a religious meaning, well-defined historically. Third, I think that it is telling that Kant defined this incapacity by a certain correlation between the exercise of an authority which maintains humanity in this minority condition, the correlation between this excess of authority and, on the other hand, something that he considers, that he calls a lack of decision and courage. And consequently, this definition of the *Aufklärung* is not simply going to be a kind of historical and speculative definition. In this definition of the *Aufklärung*, there will be something which no doubt it may be a little ridiculous to call a sermon, and yet it is very much a call for courage that he sounds in this description of the *Aufklärung*. One should not forget that it was a newspaper article. There is much work to be done on the relationship between philosophy and journalism from the end of the 18th century on, a study.... Unless it has already been done, but I am not sure of that.... It is very interesting to see from what point on philosophers intervene in newspapers in order to say something that is for them philosophically interesting and which, nevertheless, is inscribed in a certain relationship to the public which they intend to mobilize. And finally, it is characteristic that, in this text on the *Aufklärung,* Kant precisely gives religion, law and knowledge as examples of maintaining humanity in the minority condition and consequently as examples of points where the *Aufklärung* must lift this minority condition and in some way majoritize men. What Kant was describing as the *Aufklärung* is very much what I was trying before to describe as critique, this critical attitude which appears as a specific attitude in the Western world starting with what was historically, I believe, the great process of society's governmentalization. And in relation to this *Aufklärung* (whose motto you know and Kant reminds us is *"sapere aude,"* to which Frederick II countered: "Let them reason all they want to as long as they obey") in any case, in relation to this *Aufklärung,* how will Kant define critique? Or, in any case, since I am not attempting to recoup Kant's entire critical project in all its philosophical rigor...I would not allow myself to do so before such an audience of philosophers, since I myself am not a philosopher and barely a critic...in terms of this *Aufklärung,* how is one going to situate what is understood by *critique*? If Kant actually calls in this whole critical movement which preceded the *Aufklärung*, how is one going to situate what *he* understands as critique. I will say, and these are completely childish things, that in relation to the *Aufklärung*, in Kant's eyes, critique will be what he is going to say to knowledge: do you know up to what point you can know? Reason as much as you want, but do you really know up to what point you can reason without it becoming dangerous? Critique will say, in short, that it is not so much a matter of what we are undertaking, more or less courageously, than it is the idea we have of our knowledge and its limits. Our liberty is at stake and consequently, instead of letting someone else say "obey," it is at this point, once one has gotten an adequate idea of one's own knowledge and its limits, that the principle of autonomy can be discovered. One will then no longer have to hear the *obey;* or rather, the *obey* will be founded on autonomy itself.

I am not attempting to show the opposition there may be between Kant's analysis of the *Aufklärung* and his critical project. I think it would be easy to show that for Kant himself, this true courage to know which was put forward by the *Aufklärung*, this same courage to know involved recognizing the limits of knowledge. It would also be easy to show that, for Kant, autonomy is not at all opposed to obeying the sovereign. Nevertheless, in his attempt to desubjugate the subject in the context of power and truth, as a prolegomena to the whole present and future *Aufklärung*, Kant set forth critique's primordial responsibility, to know knowledge.

***

I would not like to insist any further on the implications of this kind of gap between *Aufklärung* and critique that Kant wanted to indicate. I would simply like to insist on this historical aspect of the problem which is suggested to us by what happened in the 19th century. The history of the 19th century offered a greater opportunity to pursue the critical enterprise that Kant had in some way situated at a distance from the *Aufklärung*, than it did for something like the *Aufklärung* itself. In other words, 19th century history—and, of course, 20th century history, even more so—seem to have to side with Kant or at least provide a concrete hold on this new critical attitude, this critical attitude set back from the *Aufklärung,* and which Kant had made possible.

This historical hold, seemingly afforded much more to Kantian critique than to the courage of the *Aufklärung*, was characterized very simply by the following three basic features: first, positivist science, that is to say, it basically had confidence in itself, even when it remained carefully critical of each one of its results; second, the development of a State or a state system which justified itself as the reason and deep rationality of history and which, moreover, selected as its instruments procedures to rationalize the economy and society; and hence, the third feature, this stitching together of scientific positivism and the development of States, a science of the State, or a statism, if you like. A fabric of tight relationships is woven between them such that science is going to play an increasingly determinant part in the development of productive forces and, such that, in addition, state-type powers are going to be increasingly exercised through refined techniques. Thus, the fact that the 1784 question, *What is Aufkläung?*, or rather the way in which Kant, in terms of this question and the answer he gave it, tried to situate his critical enterprise, this questioning about the relationships between *Aufklärung* and *Critique* is going to legitimately arouse suspicion or, in any case, more and more skeptical questioning: for what excesses of power, for what governmentalization, all the more impossible to evade as it is reasonably justified, is reason not itself historically responsible?

Moreover, I think that the future of this question was not exactly the same in Germany and in France for historical reasons which should be analyzed because they are complex.

Roughly, one can say this: it is less perhaps because of the recent development of the beautiful, all-new and rational State in Germany than due to a very old attachment of the Universities to the *Wissenschaft* and to administrative and state structures, that there is this suspicion that something in rationalization and maybe even in reason itself is responsible for excesses of power, well, then!: it seems to me that this suspicion was especially well-developed in Germany and let us say to make it short, that it was especially developed within what we could call the German Left. In any case, from the Hegelian Left to the Frankfurt School, there has been a complete critique of positivism, objectivism, rationalization, of *technè* and technicalization, a whole critique of the relationships between the fundamental project of science and techniques whose objective was to show the connections between science's naive presumptions, on one hand, and the forms of domination characteristic of contemporary society, on the other. To cite the example presumably the most distant from what could be called a Leftist critique, we should recall that Husserl, in 1936, referred the contemporary crisis of European humanity to something that involved the relationships between knowledge and technique, from *épistèmè* to *technè*.

In France, the conditions for the exercise of philosophy and political reflection were very different. And because of this, the critique of presumptuous reason and its specific effects of power do not seem to have been directed in the same way. And it would be, I think, aligned with a certain kind of thinking on the Right, during the 19th and 20th centuries, where one can again find this same historical indictment of reason or rationalization in the name of the effects of power that it carries along with it. In any case, the block constituted by the Enlightenment and the Revolution has no doubt prevented us in a general way from truly and profoundly questioning this relationship between rationalization and power. Perhaps it is also because the Reformation, that is to say, what I believe was a very deeply rooted, first critical movement of the art of not being governed, the fact that the Reformation did not have the same degree of expansion and success in France as it had in Germany, clearly shows that in France this notion of the *Aufklärung*, with all the problems it posed, was not as widely accepted, and moreover, never became as influential a historical reference as it did in Germany. Let us say that in France, we were satisfied with a certain political valorization of the 18th century philosophers even though Enlightenment thought was disqualified as a minor episode in the history of philosophy. In Germany, on the contrary, the *Aufklärung* was certainly understood, for better or worse, it doesn'st matter, as an important episode, a sort of brilliant manifestation of the profound destination of Western reason. In the *Aufklärung* and in the whole period that runs from the 16th to the 18th century and serves as the reference for this notion of *Aufklärung*, an attempt was being made to decipher and recognize the most accentuated slope of this line of Western reason whereas it was the politics to which it was linked that became the object of suspicious examination. This is, if you will, roughly the chasm between France and Germany in terms of the way the problem of the *Aufklärung* was posed during the 19th and the first half of the 20th century.

I do believe that the situation in France has changed in recent years. It seems to me that in France, in fact, (just as the problem of the

Aufklärung had been so important in German thought since Mendelssohn, Kant, through Hegel, Nietzsche, Husserl, the Frankfurt School, etc...) an era has arrived where precisely this problem of the *Aufklärung* can be re-approached in significant proximity to the work of the Frankfurt School. Let us say, once again to be brief—and it comes as no surprise—that the question of what the *Aufklärung* is has returned to us through phenomenology and the problems it raised. Actually, it has come back to us through the question of meaning and what can constitute meaning. How it is that meaning could be had out of nonsense? How does meaning occur? This is a question which clearly is the complement to another: how is it that the great movement of rationalization has led us to so much noise, so much furor, so much silence and so many sad mechanisms? After all, we shouldn't forget that *La Nausée* is more or less contemporaneous with the *Krisis*. And it is through the analysis, after the war, of the following, that meaning is being solely constituted by systems of constraints characteristic of the signifying machinery. It seems to me that it is through the analysis of this fact whereby meaning only exists through the effects of coercion which are specific to these structures that, by a strange short-cut, the problem between *ratio* and *power* was rediscovered. I also think (and this would definitely be a study to do) that—analyzing the history of science, this whole problematization of the history of the sciences (no doubt also rooted in phenomenology which, in France, by way of Cavaillès, via Bachelard and through Georges Canguilhem, belongs to another history altogether)—the historical problem of the historicity of the sciences has some relationships to and analogies with and echoes, to some degree, this problem of the constitution of meaning. How is this rationality born? How is it formed from something which is totally different from it? There we have the reciprocal and inverse problem of that of the *Aufklärung*: how is it that rationalization leads to the furor of power?

So it seems that whether it be the research on the constitution of meaning with the discovery that meaning is only constituted by the coercive structures of the signifier or analyses done on the history of scientific rationality with the effects of constraint linked to its institutionalization and the constitution of models, all this, all this historical research has done, I believe, is break in like a ray of morning light through a kind of narrow academic window to merge into what was, after all, the deep undertow of our history for the past century. For all the claim that our social and economic organization lacked rationality, we found ourselves facing I don't know if it's too much or too little reason, but in any case surely facing too much power. For all the praises we lavished on the promises of the revolution, I don't know if it is a good or a bad thing where it actually occurred, but we found ourselves faced with the inertia of a power which was maintaining itself indefinitely. And for all our vindication of the opposition between ideologies of violence and the veritable scientific theory of society, that of the proletariat and of history, we found ourselves with two forms of power that resembled each other like two brothers: Fascism and Stalinism. Hence, the question returns: what is the *Aufklärung*? Consequently, the series of problems which distinguished the analyses of Max Weber is reactivated: where are we with this rationalization which can be said to characterize not only Western thought and science since the 16th century, but also social relationships, state organizations, economic practices and perhaps even individual behaviors? What about this rationalization with its effects of constraint and maybe of obnubilation, of the never radically contested but still all massive and ever-growing establishment of a vast technical and scientific system?

This problem, for which in France we must now shoulder the responsibility, is this problem of

what is the *Aufklärung?* We can approach it in different ways. And the way in which I would like to
approach this — you should trust me about it — is
absolutely not evoked here to be critical or polemical. For these two reasons I am seeking nothing
else than to point out differences and somehow see
up to what point we can multiply them, disseminate them, and distinguish them in terms of each
other, displacing, if you will, the forms of analyses
of this *Aufklärung* problem, which is perhaps, after
all, the problem of modern philosophy.

In tackling this problem which shows our fel-
lowship with the Frankfurt School, I would like,
in any case, to immediately note that making the
Aufklärung the central question definitely means a
number of things. First, it means that we are
engaging a certain historical and philosophical
practice which has nothing to do with the philosophy of history or the history of philosophy. It is
a certain historical-philosophical practice, and by
that I mean that the domain of experience referred
to by this philosophical work in no way excludes
any other. It is neither inner experience, nor the
fundamental structures of scientific knowledge. It
is also not a group of historical contents elaborated elsewhere, treated by historians and received
as ready-made facts. Actually, in this historical-

philosophical practice, one has to make one's own history, fabricate history, as if through fiction, in terms of how it would be traversed by the question of the relationships between structures of rationality which articulate true discourse and the mechanisms of subjugation which are linked to it. This is evidently a question which displaces the historical objects familiar to historians towards the problem of the subject and the truth about which historians are not usually concerned. We also see that this question invests philosophical work, philosophical thought and the philosophical analysis in empirical contents designed by it. It follows, if you will, that historians faced with this historical or philosophical work are going to say: "yes, of course, yes, maybe." In any case, it is never exactly right, given the effect of interference due to the displacement toward the subject and the truth about which I was speaking. And even if they don't take on an air of offended guinea-fowls, philosophers generally think: "philosophy, in spite of everything, is something else altogether." And this is due to the effect of falling, of returning to an empiricity which is not even grounded in inner experience.

Let us grant these sideline voices all the importance they deserve, and it is indeed a great deal of

importance. They indicate at least negatively that
we are on the right path, and by this I mean that
through the historical contents that we elaborate
and to which we adhere because they are true or
because they are valued as true, the question is
being raised: "what, therefore, am I," I who belong
to this humanity, perhaps to this piece of it, at this
point in time, at this instant of humanity which is
subjected to the power of truth in general and truths
in particular? The first characteristic of this historical-philosophical practice, if you will, is to desub-
jectify the philosophical question by way of historical contents, to liberate historical contents by examining the effects of power whose truth affects them
and from which they supposedly derive. In addition, this historical-philosophical practice is clearly
found in the privileged relationship to a certain period which can be determined empirically. Even if it
is   relatively   and   necessarily   vague,   the
Enlightenment period is certainly designated as a
formative stage for modern humanity. This is the
Aufklärung in the wide sense of the term to which
Kant, Weber, etc. referred, a period without fixed
dates, with multiple points of entry since one can
also define it by the formation of capitalism, the constitution of the bourgeois world, the establishment
of state systems, the foundation of modern science

with all its correlative techniques, the organization
of a confrontation between the art of being governed and that of not being quite so governed.
Consequently, this is a privileged period for historical-philosophical work, since these relationships
between power, truth and the subject appear live on
the surface of visible transformations. Yet it is also a
privilege in the sense that one has to form a matrix
from it in order to transit through a whole series of
other possible domains. Let us say, if you will, that
it is not because we privilege the 18th century,
because we are interested in it, that we encounter
the problem of the *Aufklärung*. I would say instead
that it is because we fundamentally want to ask the
question, *What is Aufklärung?* that we encounter the
historical scheme of our modernity. The point is not
to say that the Greeks of the 5th century are a little
like the philosophers of the 18th or that the 12th
century was already a kind of Renaissance, but
rather to try to see under what conditions, at the
cost of which modifications or generalizations we
can apply this question of the *Aufklärung* to any
moment in history, that is, the question of the relationships between power, truth and the subject.

Such is the general framework of this research
I would call historical-philosophical. Now we will
see how we can conduct it.

***

I was saying before that I wanted in any case to very vaguely trace possible tracks other than those which seemed to have been up till now most willingly cleared. This in no way accuses the latter of leading nowhere or of not providing any valid results. I would simply like to say and suggest the following: it seems to me that this question of the *Aufklärung*, since Kant, because of Kant, and presumably because of this separation he introduced between *Aufklärung* and *critique,* was essentially raised in terms of knowledge (*connaissance*), that is, by starting with what was the historical destiny of knowledge at the time of the constitution of modern science. Also, by looking for what in this destiny already indicated the indefinite effects of power to which this question was necessarily going to be linked through objectivism, positivism, technicism, etc., by connecting this knowledge with the conditions of the constitution and legitimacy of all possible knowledge, and finally, by seeing how the exit from legitimacy (illusion, error, forgetting, recovery, etc.) occurred in history. In a word, this is the procedure of analysis that seems to me to have been deeply mobilized by the gap

between *critique* and *Aufklärung* engineered by
Kant. I believe that from this point on, we see a
procedure of analysis which is basically the one
most often followed, an analytical procedure
which could be called an investigation into the
legitimacy of historical modes of knowing (*connaître*). It is in this way, in any case, that many 18th
century philosophers understood it, it is also how
Dilthey, Habermas, etc. understood it. Still, more
simply put: what false idea has knowledge gotten
of itself and what excessive use has it exposed itself
to, to what domination is it therefore linked?

Well, now! Rather than this procedure which
takes shape as an investigation into the legitimacy of historical modes of knowing, we can perhaps envision a different procedure. It may take
the question of the *Aufklärung* as its way of gaining access, not to the problem of knowledge, but
to that of power. It would proceed not as an
investigation into legitimacy, but as something I
would call an examination of *"eventualization"*
(*événementialisation*). Forgive me for this horrible
word! And, right away, what does it mean? What
I understand by the procedure of eventualization,
whilst historians cry out in grief, would be the
following: first, one takes groups of elements
where, in a totally empirical and temporary way,

connections between mechanisms of coercion and contents of knowledge can be identified. Mechanisms of different types of coercion, maybe also legislative elements, rules, material set-ups, authoritative phenomena, etc. One would also consider the contents of knowledge in terms of their diversity and heterogeneity, view them in the context of the effects of power they generate in as much as they are validated by their belonging to a system of knowledge. We are therefore not attempting to find out what is true or false, founded or unfounded, real or illusory, scientific or ideological, legitimate or abusive. What we are trying to find out is what are the links, what are the connections that can be identified between mechanisms of coercion and elements of knowledge, what is the interplay of relay and support developed between them, such that a given element of knowledge takes on the effects of power in a given system where it is allocated to a true, probable, uncertain or false element, such that a procedure of coercion acquires the very form and justifications of a rational, calculated, technically efficient element, etc.

Therefore, on this first level, there is no case made here for the attribution of legitimacy, no assigning points of error and illusion.

And this is why, at this level, it seems to me that one can use two words whose function is not to designate entities, powers (*puissances*) or something like transcendentals, but rather to perform a systematic reduction of value for the domains to which they refer, let us say, a neutralization concerning the effects of legitimacy and an elucidation of what makes them at some point acceptable and in fact, had them accepted. Hence, the use of the word knowledge (*savoir*) that refers to all procedures and all effects of knowledge (*connaissance*) which are acceptable at a given point in time and in a specific domain; and secondly, the term power (*pouvoir*) which merely covers a whole series of particular mechanisms, definable and defined, which seem likely to induce behaviors or discourses. We see right away that these two terms only have a methodological function. It is not a matter of identifying general principles of reality through them, but of somehow pinpointing the analytical front, the type of element that must be pertinent for the analysis. It is furthermore a matter of preventing the perspective of legitimation from coming into play as it does when the terms knowledge (*connaissance*) or domination are used. It is also important, at every stage in the analysis, to be able to give knowledge and power a precise and determined content: such and such an element of knowledge, such and such a mechanism of power. No one should ever think that there exists *one* knowledge or *one* power, or worse, *knowledge* or *power* which would operate in and of themselves. Knowledge and power are only an analytical grid. We also see that this grid is not made up of two categories with elements which are foreign to one another, with what would be from knowledge on one side and what would be from power, on the other—and what I was saying before about them made them exterior to one another—for nothing can exist as an element of knowledge if, on one hand, it is does not conform to a set of rules and constraints characteristic, for example, of a given type of scientific discourse in a given period, and if, on the other hand, it does not possess the effects of coercion or simply the incentives peculiar to what is scientifically validated or simply rational or simply generally accepted, etc. Conversely, nothing can function as a mechanism of power if it is not deployed according to procedures, instruments, means, and objectives which can be validated in more or less coherent systems of knowledge. It is therefore not a matter of describing what knowledge is and what power is and how one would repress the other or how the other would abuse the one, but rather, a nexus of knowledge-power has to be described so that we can grasp what constitutes the acceptability of a system, be it the mental health system, the penal system, delinquency, sexuality, etc.

In short, it seems that from the empirical observability for us of an ensemble to its historical acceptability, to the very period of time during which it is actually observable, the route goes by way of an analysis of the knowledge-power nexus supporting it, recouping it at the point where it is accepted, moving toward what makes it acceptable, of course, not in general, but only where it is accepted. This is what can be characterized as recouping it in its positivity. Here, then, is a type of procedure which, unconcerned with legitimizing and consequently, excluding the fundamental point of view of the law, runs through the cycle of positivity by proceeding from the fact of acceptance to the system of acceptability analyzed through the knowledge-power interplay. Let us say that this is, approximately, the *archeological* level.

Secondly, one sees right away from this type of analysis that there are several dangers which cannot fail to appear as its negative and costly consequences.

These positivities are ensembles which are not

at all obvious in the sense that whatever habits or routines may have made them familiar to us, whatever the blinding force of the power mechanisms they call into play or whatever justifications they may have developed, they were not made acceptable by any originally existing right. And what must be extracted in order to fathom what could have made them acceptable is precisely that they were not at all obvious, that they were not inscribed in any *a priori*, nor contained in any precedent. There are two correlative operations to perform: bring out the conditions of acceptability of a system and follow the breaking points which indicate its emergence. It was not at all obvious that madness and mental illness were superimposed in the institutional and scientific system of psychiatry. It was not a given either that punishment, imprisonment and penitentiary discipline had come to be articulated in the penal system. It was also not a given that desire, concupiscence and individuals' sexual behavior had to actually be articulated one upon the other in a system of knowledge and normality called sexuality. The identification of the acceptability of a system cannot be dissociated from identifying what made it difficult to accept: its arbitrary nature in terms of knowledge, its violence in terms of power, in short, its energy. Hence, it is necessary to take responsibility for this structure in order to better account for its artifices.

The second consequence is also costly and negative for these ensembles are not analyzed as universals to which history, with its particular circumstances, would add a number of modifications. Of course, many accepted elements, many conditions of acceptability may have a long history, but what has to be recovered in some way through the analysis of these positivities are not incarnations of an essence, or individualizations of a species, but rather, pure singularities: the singularity of madness in the modern Western world, the absolute singularity of sexuality, the absolute singularity of our moral-legal system of punishment.

There is no foundational recourse, no escape within a pure form. This is, without a doubt, one of the most important and debatable aspects of this historical-philosophical approach. If it neither wants to swing toward the philosophy of history, nor toward historical analysis, then it has to keep itself within the field of immanence of pure singularities. Then what? Rupture, discontinuity, singularity, pure description, still tableau, no explanation, dead-end, you know all that. One may say that the analysis of positivities does not partake in these so-called explicative procedures to which are attributed causal value according to three conditions:

1) causal value is only recognized in explanations targeting a final authority, valorized as a profound and unique agency; for some, it is economics; for others, demography;

2) causal value is only recognized for that which obeys a pyramid formation pointing towards the cause or causal focus, the unitary origin;

3) and, finally, causal value is only recognized for that which establishes a certain unavoidability, or at least, that which approaches necessity.

The analysis of positivities, to the degree that these are pure singularities which are assigned not to a species or an essence, but to simple conditions of acceptability, well then, this analysis requires the deployment of a complex and tight causal network, but presumably of another kind, the kind which would not obey this requirement of being saturated by a deep, unitary, pyramidal and necessary principle. We have to establish a network which accounts for this singularity as an effect. Hence there is a need for a multiplicity of relationships, a differentiation between different types of relationships, between different forms of necessity among connections, a deciphering of circular interactions and actions taking into account the intersection of heterogeneous processes. There is, therefore, nothing more foreign to such an analysis than the rejection of causality. Nevertheless, what is very important is not that such analyses bring a whole group of derived phenomena back to a cause, but rather that they are capable of making a singular positivity intelligible precisely in terms of that which makes it singular.

Let us say, roughly, that as opposed to a genesis oriented towards the unity of some principial cause burdened with multiple descendants, what is proposed instead is a *genealogy*, that is, something that attempts to restore the conditions for the appearance of a singularity born out of multiple determining elements of which it is not the product, but rather the effect. A process of making it intelligible but with the clear understanding that this does not function according to any principle of closure. There is no principle of closure for several reasons.

The first is that this singular effect can be accounted for in terms of relationships which are, if not totally, at least predominantly, relationships of interactions between individuals or groups. In other words, these relationships involve subjects, types of behavior, decisions and choices. It is not in the nature of things that we are likely to find support. Support for this network of intelligible relationships is in the logic inherent to the context of interactions with its always variable margins of non-certainty.

There is also no closure because the relationships we are attempting to establish to account for a singularity as an effect, this network of relationships must not make up one plane only. These relationships are in perpetual slippage from one another. At a given level, the logic of interactions operates between individuals who are able to respect its singular effects, both its specificity and its rules, while managing along with other elements interactions operating at another level, such that, in a way, none of these interactions appears to be primary or absolutely totalizing. Each interaction can be re-situated in a context that exceeds it and conversely, however local it may be, each has an effect or possible effect on the interaction to which it belongs and by which it is enveloped. Therefore, schematically speaking, we have perpetual mobility, essential fragility or rather the complex interplay between what replicates the same process and what transforms it. In short, here we would have to bring out a whole form of analyses which could be called *strategics*.

In speaking of archeology, strategy and genealogy, I am not thinking of three successive levels which would be derived, one from the other, but of characterizing three necessarily contemporaneous dimensions in the same analysis. These three dimensions, by their very simultaneity, should allow us to recoup whatever positivities there are, that is, those conditions which make acceptable a singularity whose intelligibility is established by identifying interactions and strategies within which it is integrated. It is such research accounting for... [*a few sentences are missing here where the tape was turned over*]... produced as an effect, and finally *eventualization* in that we have to deal with something whose stability, deep rootedness and foundation is never such that we cannot in one way or another envisage, if not its disappearance then at least, identifying by what and from what its disappearance is possible.

I was saying before that instead of defining the problem in terms of knowledge and legitimation, it was necessary to approach the question in terms of power and eventualization. As you see, one does not have to work with power understood as domination, as mastery, as a fundamental given, a unique principle, explanation or irreducible law. On the contrary, it always has to be considered in relation to a field of interactions, contemplated in a relationship which cannot be dissociated from forms of knowledge. One always has to think about it in such a way as to see how it is associated with a domain of possibility and consequently, of reversibility, of possible reversal.

Thus you see that the question is no longer through what error, illusion, oversight, or illegitimacy has knowledge come to induce effects of domination manifested in the modern world by the hegemony of [*inaudible*]. The question instead would be: how can the indivisibility of knowledge and power in the context of interactions and multiple strategies induce both singularities, fixed according to their conditions of acceptability, and a field of possibles, of openings, indecisions, reversals and possible dislocations which make them fragile, temporary, and which turn these effects into events, nothing more, nothing less than events? In what way can the effects of coercion characteristic of these positivities not be dissipated by a return to the legitimate destination of knowledge and by a reflection on the transcendental or semi-transcendental that fixes knowledge, but how can they instead be reversed or released from within a concrete strategic field, this concrete strategic field that induced them, starting with this decision not to be governed?

In conclusion, given the movement which swung critical attitude over into the question of critique or better yet, the movement responsible for reassessing the *Aufklärung* enterprise within the critical project whose intent was to allow knowledge to acquire an adequate idea of itself — given this swinging movement, this slippage, this way of deporting the question of the *Aufklärung* into critique — might it not now be necessary to follow the opposite route? Might we not try to travel this road, but in the opposite direction? And if it is necessary to ask the question about knowledge in its relationship to domination, it would be, first and foremost, from a certain decision-making will not to be governed, the decision-making will, both an individual and collective attitude which meant, as Kant said, to get out of one's minority. A question of attitude. You see now why I could not, did not dare, give a title to my conference since if I had, it would have been: "What is the *Aufklärung*?"

GOUHIER: I thank Michel Foucault very much for having given us such a well-coordinated group of reflections which I would call philosophical, although he said *not being a philosopher myself.* I have to say right away that after having said "not being a philosopher myself," he added "barely a critic," that is to say, anyway, a bit of a critic. And after his presentation I wonder if being a bit of a critic is not being very much a philosopher.

NOËL MOULOUD: I would like to make, perhaps, two or three remarks. The first is the following: Mr. Foucault seems to have confronted us with
a general attitude of thought, the refusal of power
or the refusal of the constraining rule which engen-
ders a general attitude, a critical attitude. He went
from there to a problematics that he presented as
an extension of this attitude, an actualization of this
attitude. These are problems which are presently
raised concerning the relationships of knowledge,
technology and power. I would see, in a way, local-
ized critical attitudes, revolving around certain core
problems with, that is to say, to a great extent,
sources or, if you will, historical limits. We first
have to have a practice, a method which reaches
certain limits, which posits problems, which ends
up at certain impasses, in order for a critical attitude to emerge. And thus, for example, there are
the successful methodologies of positivism which,
notwithstanding the difficulties raised, have elicited
the well-known critical reactions that appeared a
half-century ago, that is to say, logicist reflection
and criticist reflection. I am thinking of the
Popperian school or Wittgensteinian school on the
limits of a normalized scientific language. Often, in
these critical periods, we see a new resolution

appear, the search for a renewed practice, for a method which itself has a regional aspect, an aspect of historical research.

FOUCAULT: You are absolutely right. It is very much in this way that the critical attitude got started and developed its consequences in a privileged manner in the 19th century. I would say that this is precisely the Kantian channel, that the strong period, the essential phase of critical attitude should be the problem of questioning knowledge on its own limits or impasses, if you like, which it encounters in its primary and concrete exercise.

Two things struck me. On one hand, if you like, this Kantian use of critical attitude — and to tell the truth, in Kant, the problem is very explicitly posed — did not prevent critique from asking this question. (We can argue whether or not this is a fundamental issue.) This question is: what is the use of reason, what use of reason can carry its effects over to the abuses of the exercise of power, and consequently, to the concrete destination of liberty? I think that this problem was far from being ignored by Kant and that there was, especially in Germany, a whole movement of reflection around this theme. If you like, generalizing it some, it displaced the strict critical problem that you cited towards other regions. You cite Popper, but after all, excesses of power were also a very fundamental problem for him.

On the other hand, what I wanted to point out is that—and please forgive me for the sketchiness in all this—the history of the critical attitude, as it unfolds specifcially in the West and in the modern Western world since the 15th–16th centuries—must have its origin in the religious struggles and spiritual attitudes prevalent during the second half of the Middle Ages, precisely at the time when the problem was posed: how should one be governed, is one going to accept being governed like that? It is then that things are at their most concrete level, the most historically determined: all the struggles around the pastoral during the second half of the Middle Ages prepared the way for the Reformation and, I think, were the kind of historical limit upon which this critical attitude developed.

HENRI BIRAULT: I do not wish to play the upset guinea-fowl here! I completely agree with the way in which the question of the *Aufklärung* was explicitly taken over by Kant in order to simultaneously undergo a decisive theoretical restriction in terms of the moral, religious and political imperatives, etc., which are characteristic of Kant's philosophy.

I think that we are in total agreement on this point.

Now, concerning the more directly positive part of the exposition, when it was a matter of studying the crossfire between knowledge and power, on the ground level, somehow on the level of the event, I wonder if there still is not some space there all the same for an underlying question and, let us say, one which is more essentially or traditionally philosophical and would be a backdrop to this precious and minute study of the interplay between knowledge and power in different areas. This metaphysical and historical question might be formulated in the following way: can we not say that at a point in our history and in a certain region of the world, knowledge in and of itself, knowledge as such, took on the form of a power (*pouvoir*) or a potency (*puissance*) while on the side of power, always defined as a *savoir-faire*, a certain way of knowing how to take or how to take on something finally manifested the properly dynamic essence of the noetic? It comes as no surprise that this had to be so and that Michel Foucault is then able to find and disentangle the networks or multiple relations established between knowledge and power since at least from a certain period on, knowledge is down deep a power, and power down deep a knowledge, knowledge and power of the same will, of the same will I must call a will to power.

FOUCAULT: Would your question be about the generality of this type of relationship?

BIRAULT: Not so much its generality as its radicality or occult foundation this side of the duality of the two terms knowledge–power. Is it not possible to rediscover a sort of common essence of knowledge and power, knowledge defining itself as knowledge of power and power defining itself as knowledge of power (to then carefully explore the multiple meaning of this double genitive)?

FOUCAULT: Absolutely. I was insufficiently clear about this very point, in as much as what I would like to do, what I was suggesting, is above or below a kind of description. Roughly, there are intellectuals and men in power, there are scientists and the requirements of industry, etc. In fact, we have an entirely interwoven network. Not only with elements of knowledge and power; but for knowledge to function as knowledge it must exercise a power. Within other discourses of knowledge in relation to discourses of possible knowledge, each statement considered true exerts a certain power and it creates, at the same time, a possibility. Inversely, all exercise of power, even if it is a question of putting someone to death, implies at least a *savoir-faire.* And, after all, to savagely crush an individual is also a way of taking something on. Therefore, if you will, I completely agree and this is what I was trying to bring out: there is a kind of shimmering under the polarities which, to us, seem very distinct from those of power....

MOULOUD: I return to our common reference, for both Mr. Birault and myself: Popper. One of Popper's intentions is to show that in the constitution of spheres of power, whatever their nature, that is, dogmas, imperative norms, paradigms, it is not knowledge itself which is active and responsible, but a deviant rationality which is no longer truly knowledge. Knowledge—or rationality, inasmuch as it is formative, itself stripped of paradigms, stripped of recipes. On its own initiative it questions its own assurances, its own authority and engages in a "polemics against itself." It is precisely for this reason that it is indeed rationality, and the methodology Popper conceives of is to separate these two behaviors, to decide between them in order to make any confusion or mixture impossible between the use of recipes, the management of procedures and the invention of reasons. And I would wonder, although it is more difficult, if in the human, social, historical domain, social sciences as a whole are not equally and primarily responsible for this opening; yet, it is a very difficult situation because social sciences are, in fact, allied with technology. Between a science and the powers that use it, there is a relationship which is not truly essential; although important, it remains "contingent" in a certain way. The technical conditions for the use of knowledge are in a more direct relationship with the exercise of a power, a power which dodges exchange or examination, rather than the conditions of knowledge itself. And it is in this sense that I do not altogether understand the argument. Otherwise, Mr. Foucault made some enlightening remarks which he will surely develop. But I ask myself the question: is there a really direct link between the obligations or requirements of knowledge and those of power?

FOUCAULT: I would be thrilled if one could do it like that, that is, if one could say: there is a good science, one which is both true and does not partake of nasty power; and then obviously the bad use of science, either in its opportunistic application or in its errors. If you can prove to me that this is the case, then, well! I will leave here happy.

MOULOUD: I am not saying as much. I recognize that the historical connection, the factual link is strong. But I observe several things: that new scientific investigations (those in biology, the social sciences) are again putting man and society in a situation of non-determination, opening up inroads to liberty for them, and thus constraining them, to put it this way, to once again making decisions. Besides that, oppressive powers rarely rely on scientific knowledge, but prefer to rely on non-knowledge, a science which has first been reduced to a "myth." Racism founded on a "pseudo-genetics" or political pragmatism founded on a neo-Lamarckian deformation of biology are familiar examples. And finally, I also understand very well that a science's positive information calls for the distance of critical judgment. Yet it seems to me — and this was approximately my argument — that humanist critique, which assumes cultural and axiological criteria, cannot be entirely developed or succeed without the support that knowledge brings to it, criticizing its bases, its presuppositions and its antecedents. This especially concerns explanations provided by the human sciences and history. And it seems to me that Habermas, in particular, includes this analytic dimension in what he calls the critique of ideologies, even of those very ones engendered by knowledge.

FOUCAULT: I think that this is precisely the advantage of critique!

GOUHIER: I would like to ask you a question. I completely agree with your historical distinctions and the importance of the Reformation. But it seems to me that throughout all of Western tradition, there is a critical ferment due to Socratic thought. I wanted to ask you if the word *critique* as you defined it and used it, could not be an appropriate term with which to call what I would provisionally label a critical ferment of Socratism in Western thought, which played a role in the 16th and 17th centuries with the return to Socrates?

FOUCAULT: You confront me with a more difficult question. I will say that the return to Socratism (we feel it, identify it, see it historically, it seems, between the 16th and 17th centuries) was only possible in the context of these, for me far more important, issues which were the pastoral struggles and this problem of governing men, using the term government in the very full and broad meaning that it had at the end of the Middle Ages. To govern men was to take them by the hand and lead them to their salvation through an operation, a technique of precise piloting, which implied a full range of knowledge concerning the individual being guided, the truth towards which one was guiding....

GOUHIER: Would you be able to do your analysis all over again if you were giving a paper on Socrates and his times?

FOUCAULT: This indeed is the real problem. Here again, I am responding rapidly to something rather difficult. It seems to me that fundamentally when one investigates Socrates like that, or rather —I dare not say it—I wonder if Heidegger investigating the Presocratics doesn't do it... no, not at all, it is not at all a matter of resorting to anachronism and of projecting the 18th century on the 5th.... But this question of the *Aufklärung* which is, I think, quite fundamental for Western philosophy since Kant, I wonder if it is not a question which somehow scans all possible history down to the radical origins of philosophy. In this light, the trial of Socrates can, I think, be investigated in a valid manner, without any anachronism, but starting with a problem which is and which was, in any case, perceived by Kant as the problem of the *Aufklärung*.

JEAN-LOUIS BRUCH: I would like to ask a question about an expression which is central to your presentation, but which was formulated in two ways which seemed different to me. At the end, you spoke of "the decision-making will not to be governed" as a foundation or a reversal of the *Aufklärung* which was the subject of your talk. In the beginning, you spoke of "not being governed *like that*," of "not being governed so much," of "not being governed at such a price." In one case, the expression is absolute, in the other, it is relative, and according to what criteria? Is it because of having felt the abuse of governmentalization that you come to the radical position, "the decision-making will not to be governed?" I am asking this question, and finally, doesn't this last position need to be in turn the object of an investigation, a questioning that would, in essence, be philosophical?

FOUCAULT: Two good questions. On the point you raise about the variations in the expressions: I do not think that the will not to be governed at all is something that one could consider an originary aspiration. I think that, in fact, the will not to be governed is always the will not to be governed thusly, like that, by these people, at this price. As for the expression of not being governed *at all*, I believe it is the philosophical and theoretical paroxysm of something that would be this will not to be relatively governed. And when at the end I was saying "decision-making will not to be governed," then there, an error on my part, it was not to be governed thusly, like that, in this way. I was not referring to something that would be a fundamental anarchism, that would be like an originary freedom, absolutely and wholeheartedly resistant to any governmentalization. I did not say it, but this does not mean that I absolutely exclude it. I think that my presentation stops at this point, because it was already too long, but also because I am wondering... if one wants to explore this dimension of critique that seems to me to be so important because it is both part of, and not a part of, philosophy. If we were to explore this dimension of critique, would we not then find that it is supported by something akin to the historical practice of revolt, the non-acceptance of a real government, on one hand, or, on the other, the individual experience of the refusal of governmentality? What strikes me in particular—but I am perhaps haunted by this because I am working on it a lot right now—is that, if this matrix of critical attitude in the Western world must be sought out in religious attitudes and in connection with the exercise of pastoral power in the Middle Ages, all the same it is surprising that mysticism is seen as an individual experience while institutional and political struggles are viewed as absolutely unified, and in any case, constantly referring to one another. I would say that one of the first great forms of revolt in the West was mysticism. All the bastions of resistance to the authority of the Scriptures, to mediation by the pastor, were developed either in convents or outside convents by the secular population. When one sees that these experiences, these spiritual movements have very often been used as attire, vocabulary, but even more so as ways of being, and ways of supporting the hopes expressed by the struggle that we can define as economic, popular, and in Marxist terms as the struggle between the classes, I think we have here something that is quite fundamental.

In following the itinerary of this critical attitude whose history seems to begin at this point in time, should we not now investigate what the will not to be governed thusly, like that, etc., might be both as an individual and a collective experience? It is now necessary to pose the problem of will. In short, you will say that this is obvious, one cannot confront this problem, sticking closely to the theme of power without, of course, at some point, getting to the question of human will. It was so obvious that I could have realized it earlier. However, since this problem of will is a problem that Western philosophy has always treated with infinite precaution and difficulties, let us say that I tried to avoid it as much as possible. Let us say that it was unavoidable. Here I have given you some considerations on my work in progress.

ANDRÉ SERNIN: To which side do you lean more? Would it be towards August Comte, schematically speaking, who rigorously separates spiritual from temporal power or, on the contrary, towards Plato who said that things would never go well until philosophers were themselves made the leaders of temporal power?

FOUCAULT: Do I really have to choose?

SERNIN: No, you don't have to choose between them, but which one would you tend to lean to more?

FOUCAULT: I would try to inch my way out from between them!

PIERRE HADJI-DIMOU: You have successfully presented us with the problem of critique in its connection to philosophy and you have arrived at the relationships between power and knowledge. I wanted to contribute a little clarification on the subject of Greek thought. I think that the problem was already formulated by our President. "To know" (*connaître*) is to have *logos* and *mythos*. I think that with the *Aufklärung*, we are not able "to know." Knowledge is not only rationality, it is not only *logos* in historical life, there is a second source, *mythos*. If we refer to the discussion between Protagoras and Socrates, when Protagoras is asking the question about the right of the *Politeia* to punish, about its power, he says that he will specify and illustrate his thought about *mythos*. *Mythos* is linked to *logos* because there is rationality: the more it teaches us, the more beautiful it is. Here is the question I wanted to add: is it in suppressing a part of thought, irrational thought which arrives at *logos*, that is to say, is it by suppressing the *mythos* that we are able to know the sources of knowledge, the knowledge of power which also has a mythic sense to it?

FOUCAULT: I agree with your question.

SYLVAIN ZAC: I would like to make two remarks. You said, and rightly so, that critical attitude could be considered a virtue. In fact, there is a philosopher, Malebranche, who studied this virtue: it is freedom of spirit. On one hand, I do not agree with you about the relationships you establish in Kant between his article on the *Enlightenment* and his critique of knowledge. The latter obviously assigns limits, but does not itself have any limit; it is total whereas when one reads the article on the *Enlightenment,* one sees that Kant makes a very important distinction between public use and private use. In the case of public use, this courage must disappear. Which means that...

FOUCAULT: It's the opposite, since what he calls public use is...

ZAC: When someone has, for example, a tenured position in a philosophy department at a university, there, he can speak publicly and he must not criticize the Bible: on the other hand, in private, he can do so.

FOUCAULT: It's quite the contrary and that is what is so very interesting. Kant says: "there is a public use of reason which must not be limited." What is this public use? It is what circulates from scholar to scholar, appears in newspapers and publications, and appeals to everyone's conscience. These uses, these public uses of reason must not be limited, and curiously what he calls private use is, in some way, the government employee's use of reason. And the functionary or government employee, the officer, he says, does not have the right to tell his superior: "I will not obey you and your order is absurd." Curiously, what Kant defines as private use is each individual's obedience, inasmuch as he is a part of the State, to his superior, to the Sovereign or his representative.

ZAC: I agree with you. I made a mistake. Nevertheless, the result is that there are limits to the manifestation of courage in this article. And these limits, I found them all over, in all the *Aufklärer*, obviously in Mendelssohn. There is a good deal of conformist writing in the German *Aufklärung* movement which we do not find in the French *Enlightenment* of the 18th century.

FOUCAULT: I agree completely. I don't exactly see how this challenges what I said.

ZAC: I do not believe that there is an intimate historical link between the *Aufklärung* movement that you have given as a central focus and the development of critical attitude, of the attitude of resistance, from either the political or the intellectual point of view. Don't you think that we could admit this point?

FOUCAULT: I do not think, on the one hand, that Kant felt like a stranger to the *Aufklärung* which was for him his actuality and within which he was getting involved, not only through the article on the *Aufklärung*, but also in many other affairs...

ZAC: The word *Aufklärung* is found again in *Religion according to the Limits of Simple Reason*, but then it is applied to the purity of sentiments, to something internal. An inversion occurred, as with Rousseau.

FOUCAULT: I would like to finish up what I was saying.... Therefore, Kant feels perfectly connected to this present that he calls the *Aufklärung* and that he attempts to define. And regarding this movement of the *Aufklärung*, it seems to me that he introduces a dimension we can consider as more specific or, to the contrary, more general and more radical which is this: the first bold move that one must make when it is a matter of knowledge and knowing is to know what it is that one can know. This is the radicality and for Kant, moreover, the universality of his enterprise. I believe in this kinship, whatever limits, of course, the boldness of the *Aufklärer* has. I do not see how the fact that the *Aufklärer* were timid would in any way change anything in this kind of movement that Kant went through and of which, I believe, he was relatively conscious.

BIRAULT: I think that critical philosophy represents a movement which both restricts and radicalizes *Aufklärung* in general.

FOUCAULT: But its link to the *Aufklärung* was the question everyone was asking at that time. What are we saying, what is this movement that immediately preceded us and to which we still belong called the *Aufklärung*? The best proof is that it was in a newspaper that the series of articles by Mendelssohn and Kant were published.... It was a current event. A little like how we ourselves might ask the question: what is the present crisis in values?

JEANNE DUBOUCHET: I would like to ask you what material you place within knowledge. Power,

I believe I understood, since it was a matter of not being governed: but what kind of knowledge?

FOUCAULT: If I use that word it is once again essentially to neutralize everything that might either legitimize or simply hierarchize values. If you like, for me—as scandalous as this may be and must seem to be in the eyes of a scientist or a methodologist or even a historian of sciences— for me, between a statement by a psychiatrist and a mathematical operation, when I am speaking of knowledge, for now, I make no distinction between them. The only point through which I would introduce differences is to know which are the effects of power, if you like, of induction— not in the logical sense of the term—that this proposition can have, on one hand, within the sci- entific domain in which it is formulated—mathe- matics, psychiatry, etc.—and, on the other, what are the non-discursive, non-formalized, not espe- cially scientific networks of institutional power to which it is linked as soon as it is being circulated. This is what I would call knowledge (*savoir*): ele- ments of knowledge (*connaissance*) which, what- ever their value in relation to us, in relation to a pure spirit, exercise effects of power inside and outside their domain.

GOUHIER: It is my honor to thank Michel Foucault for having provided us with such an interesting session which is certain to become an especially important publication.

FOUCAULT: Thank you.

Translated by Lysa Hochroth

NOTES

1 Henri Gouhier is an historian of philosophy and a specialist in Malebranche and Bergson. Although part of the academic establishment, he remained open to new ideas (he directed Lucien Goldmann's dissertation). The discussion which follows Foucault's lecture involved various specialists in philosophy: Mouloud (aesthetics); Bruch (Kant); Zac (Spinoza); Birault (Heidegger); etc.

2 "What is an Author," first published in the *Bulletin de la Societe française de philosophie,* was translated from the French by Josue V. Harari in *Textual Strategies: Perspectives in Post-Structuralist Criticism,* edited by Josue V. Harari (Ithaca, New York: Cornell University Press, 1979). It was reprinted in *Foucault Reader,* ed. Paul Rabinow (New York: Pantheon Books, 1984).

2
What is Revolution?

It seems to me that this text reveals a new type of question in the field of philosophical reflection. Of course, it is certainly not the first text in the history of philosophy, nor is it even the only text of Kant's which gives a theme to a question concerning history. In Kant, one finds texts which examine the origins of history: the text on the beginnings of history itself, the text on the definition of the concept of race. Other texts question history on the form of its accomplishment: for example, in this same year 1784, the *Idea for a Universal History from a Cosmopolitan Point of View*. Still others discuss the internal finality which organizes historical processes, such as in the text on the use of teleological principles. All these questions, which are, moreover, tightly linked, effectively traverse Kant's analyses on the matter of history. It seems to me that the text on the *Aufklärung* is a rather different text. It does not raise any of these questions; in any case, not directly. Not the question of origin, not, despite appearances, the question of its completion, and it raises in a relatively discrete, almost lateral, way the question of the immanence of teleology to the process of history itself.

The question which, I believe, for the first time appears in this text by Kant is the question of today, the question about the present, about what is our actuality: what is happening today? What is happening right now? And what is this *right now* we all are in which defines the moment at which I am writing? It is not the first time that one finds references to the present in philosophical reflection, at least as a determined, historical situation which can have value for philosophical reflection. After all, when Descartes recounts his own itinerary in *Discours de la Méthode* and all the philosophical decisions he made, both for himself and for philosophy, he refers very explicitly to something which can be considered a historical position within the order of knowledge and sciences of his own period. Nonetheless, in these kind of references, the focus is always on finding a motive for a philosophical decision in the context of this configuration designated as the present. In Descartes, you will not find a question like: "What precisely is this present to which I belong?" Now it seems to me that the question Kant answers, that he is in fact prompted to answer, because someone had raised it, is another question. It is not simply: what in the present situation can determine this or that philosophical decision? The question is about the present and is, at first, concerned with the determination of a certain element of the present that needs to be recognized, distinguished, deciphered among all others. What is it in the present that now makes sense for philosophical reflection?

In the answer that Kant attempts to give to this line of questioning, he attempts to show how this element of the present turns out to be the carrier and the sign of a process concerning thought, bodies of knowledge and philosophy. Yet here it is a matter of showing specifically and in what ways the one who speaks as a thinker, a scientist and a philosopher is himself a part of this process and (more than that) how he has a certain role to play in this process where he will therefore find himself as both element and actor.

In short, in this text, it seems to me that one witnesses the appearance of the present as a philosophical event to which the philosopher who speaks about it belongs. If one agrees to envision philosophy as a form of discursive practice which has its own history, it seems to me that with this text on the *Aufklärung*, and I do not think that it is forcing things too much to say that for the first time, one sees philosophy problematize its own discursive actuality: an actuality that it questions as an event, as an event whose meaning, value, and philosophical singularity it has to express and in which it has to find both its own reason for being and the foundation for what it says. And in this way, one sees that for the philosopher to ask the question of how he belongs to this present is to no longer ask the question of how he belongs to a doctrine or a tradition. It will also no longer simply be a question of his belonging to a larger human community in general, but rather it will be a question of his belonging to a certain *us*, to an *us* that relates to a characteristic cultural ensemble of his own actuality.

No philosopher can go without examining his own participation in this *us* precisely because it is this *us* which is becoming the object of the philosopher's own reflection. All this, philosophy as the problematization of an actuality and the philosopher's questioning of this actuality to which he belongs and in relation to which he has to position himself, may very well characterize philosophy as a discourse of and about modernity.

Very schematically speaking, in classical culture the issue of modernity relied on an axis with two poles, antiquity and modernity. The question was formulated either in terms of an authority to be accepted or rejected (Which authority should one accept? Which model should one follow?, etc.) or still in the form (which is, moreover, the correlative of the aforementioned) of a comparative valorization: are the Ancients superior to the Moderns? Are we in a period of decadence, etc.? One sees a new manner of posing the question of modernity rise to the surface, no longer in a longitudinal relationship to the Ancients but in what could be called a *sagittal* relationship with its own present. Discourse has to reappropriate its present, on one hand, in order to again find in it its proper place, on the other, in order to express its meaning and finally, in order to specify the mode of action that it is capable of exerting within this present.

What is my actuality? What is the meaning of this actuality? And what am I doing when I speak about this actuality? I believe that this is what this new examination of modernity is all about.

It is nothing more than a path that should be explored a bit more closely. One should attempt to elaborate the genealogy, not so much of the notion of modernity, but rather of modernity as a question for examination. And, in any case, even if I take Kant's text as the point at which this question emerges, it is with the understanding that it is part of a greater historical process which should be assessed. No doubt one of the more interesting perspectives for the study of the 18th century, in general, and of the *Aufklärung*, in particular would be to examine the fact that the *Aufklärung* named itself *Aufklärung*, that it is a very unique cultural process which became aware of itself by naming itself, by situating itself in terms of its past and its future, and by indicating how it had to operate within its own present.

Is it not the *Aufklärung*, after all, the first epoch to name itself and, instead of simply characterizing itself, according to an old habit, as a period of decadence or prosperity, of splendor or misery, to name itself after a certain event that comes out of a general history of thought, reason and knowledge, and within which the epoch itself has to play its part?

The *Aufklärung* is a period, a period which set out to formulate its own motto, its own precept, and which spells out what is to be done both in relation to its present and to the forms of knowledge, ignorance and illusion in which it is capable of recognizing its historical situation.

It seems to me that this question of the *Aufklärung* provides one of the first manifestations of a certain kind of philosophizing which has had a long history over the past two centuries. It is one of the great functions of so-called modern philosophy (which would begin at the very end of the 18th century) to question itself about its own actuality.

The trajectory of this modality of philosophy throughout the 19th century up until today can be traced. The only thing that I would like to emphasize, for now, is that this question dealt with by Kant in 1784 in order to respond to a question that had been raised from the outside, Kant did not forget it. He will ask it again and he will try to answer it with regard to another event which also continually questioned itself. This event is, of course, the French Revolution.

In 1798, Kant gave a sort of follow-up to the 1784 text. In 1784, he was trying to answer the question he had been asked: "What is this *Aufklärung* of which we are a part?" and in 1798, he answers a question, that the present had confronted him with, but which had been formulated as early as 1794 by all the philosophical debate in Germany. And this question was: "What is Revolution?"

You know that *The Conflict of the Faculties* is a collection of three papers on the relationships among the different faculties that constitute the University. The second paper concerns the conflict between the School of Philosophy and the Law School. Now the whole field of relationships between philosophy and law is engrossed with the question: "Is there constant progress for humankind?" And it is in order to answer this question that Kant, in paragraph V of this paper, develops the following reasoning: if one wants to answer the question: "Is there constant progress for humankind?" then it is necessary to determine if there exists a possible cause for this progress. However, once this possibility is established, one must show that this cause effectively translates into action and for that reason elicits a certain event that shows that the cause acts in reality. To sum up, the assignment of a cause will never be able to determine anything except possible effects, or more exactly, the possibility of an effect; but the reality of an effect can only be established by the existence of an event.

Therefore, it is not enough to follow the teleological framework which makes progress possible. One must isolate an event in history that will take on the value of a sign.

A sign of what? A sign of the existence of a cause, of a permanent cause which throughout history has guided humanity on the path to progress. One must therefore show that there is a constant cause which has acted in the past, acts in the present and will act in the future. Consequently, the event that will allow us to decide if there is progress, will be a sign, *rememorativum, demonstrativum, pronosticum.* It is necessary for it to be a sign that shows that things have always been like this (the rememorative sign), a sign that clearly shows that these things are also presently happening (the demonstrative sign) and that shows, finally, that things will always happen like this (the prognostic sign). And it is in this way that we can be sure that the cause that makes progress possible has not simply acted at a given point in time but that it guarantees a general tendency of humankind in its totality to move in the direction of progress. That is the question: "Is there around us an event which would be rememorative, demonstrative and prognostic of permanent progress which carries along humankind in its totality?"

You have guessed the answer provided by Kant; but I would like to read the passage with which he introduced the Revolution as an event having the value of a sign. "Do not expect," he wrote at the beginning of paragraph VI, "this event to reside in grand gestures or major infamous acts committed by men following which what was great among men is rendered small, or what was small is rendered great, nor in ancient and brilliant buildings which disappear as if by magic while in their place others rise in some way from the depths of the earth. No, nothing like that."

In this text, Kant obviously makes an allusion to traditional reflections which sought the proof of progress or non-progress of the human species in the reversal of empires, in great catastrophes by which the most established states disappeared, in the reversal of fortunes which brought down established powers and made new ones appear. Beware, Kant cautions his readers, it is not in great events that we must look for the rememorative, demonstrative, prognostic sign of progress; it is, rather, in events that are much less grandiose, much less perceptible. We cannot analyze our own present in terms of these significant values without recodifying them in such a way that they will allow us to express the important meaning and value we are seeking for what, apparently, is without meaning and value. So what is this event which therefore is not a "great" event? There is evidently a paradox in saying that the Revolution is not a resounding event. Is it not the very example of an event that topples things over, making what was big become small, what was small become big, and swallowing up what appeared to be society's and the state's most solid structures? Yet, for Kant, it is not this aspect of the Revolution that is significant. What constitutes the event with rememorative, demonstrative and prognostic value is not the revolutionary drama itself, revolutionary exploits or the gesticulation that accompanies it. What is significant is the manner in which the Revolution turns into a spectacle, it is the way in which it is received all around by spectators who do not participate in it but who watch it, who attend the show and who, for better or worse, let themselves be dragged along by it. It is not revolutionary upheaval which constitutes the proof of progress; first of all, presumably, because it only inverts things, and also because if one had to do this revolution all over again, one would not do it. There is a very interesting passage on this: "It matters little," Kant said, "if the revolution of a people full of spirit that we have seen occur in our day" (he is thus referring to the French Revolution) "it matters little if it succeeds or fails, it matters little if it accumulates misery and atrocity, if it accumulates them to the point where a sensible man who would do it over again with the hope of bringing it to fruition would never consider, though, trying it out at this price." Therefore, it is not the revolutionary process which is important, it matters little if it succeeds or fails, this has nothing to do with progress, or at least with the sign of progress that we are seeking. The failure or success of the revolution are not signs of progress or a sign that there is no progress. But still if it were possible for someone to understand the Revolution and know how it would unfold, well realizing what the cost of this Revolution would be, this sensible man would not do it. Therefore, as "reversal," as the enterprise which can succeed or fail, as a price too heavy to pay, the Revolution in itself, cannot be considered as the sign that there exists a cause capable of sustaining the constant progress of humanity throughout history.

Instead, what makes sense and what is going to be seen as the sign of progress is that, all around the Revolution, there is, Kant says, "a sympathy of aspiration that borders on enthusiasm." What is important in the Revolution is not the Revolution itself, it is what happens in the heads of those who do not participate in it or, in any case, are not its principal actors. It is in the relationship they themselves have to this Revolution of which they are not the active agents. The enthusiasm for the Revolution is the sign, according to Kant, of humanity's moral predisposition. This predisposition is perpetually manifested in two ways: first, in the right of all people to provide themselves with the political constitution that suits them and in the principle which conforms to the law and to the moral of a political constitution such that it avoids, by virtue of its very principles, any offensive war. So it is the predisposition that carries humanity toward such a constitution which is signified by the enthusiasm for the Revolution. The Revolution as spectacle, and not as gesticulation, as a repository for the enthusiasm of those who watch it and not as the principle of upheaval for those who participate in it, is a "signum rememo-rativum," since it reveals this predisposition as originally present, it is a "signum demonstrativum" because it shows the present efficacy of this predisposition; and it is also a "signum pronosticum" since even if some results of the Revolution can be challenged, one cannot forget this predisposition that was revealed through it.

We also know very well that a political constitution willingly chosen by the people and a political constitution that avoids war are the two elements that constitute the very process of the *Aufklärung*. In other words, the Revolution is what effectively completes and continues the process of the *Aufklärung* and it is in this way as well that the

Aufklärung and the Revolution are events that can no longer be forgotten. "I uphold," writes Kant, "that, even lacking a prophetic spirit, I can make predictions for humankind based on the appearances and signs which are precursors in our period that it will reach this end, that is to say, arrive at a state such that men will be able to give themselves the constitution they want and the constitution that will prevent an offensive war so that, thereafter, this progress will no longer be challenged. Such a phenomenon in the history of humanity is no longer forgotten because it revealed a predisposition in human nature, a faculty of progressing such that no amount of political subtlety would have been able to change the course of events, only nature and liberty, brought together in the human species according to the internal principles of law, were able to announce it, albeit vaguely, as a contingent event. But if the objective aimed at by this event had not yet been reached when even the Revolution or the reform of the constitution of a people would have finally failed, or even if, after a certain amount of time, everything would once again fall into the previous old rut, as many politicians predict today, this philosophical prophecy would lose nothing of its force. For this event is too important, too deeply enmeshed in the interests of humanity and of such vast influence on the whole world not to have to be called to the people's memory on favorable occasions and recalled during crises when there are new attempts of this kind. For in a matter of such great importance for the human species, it is necessary, at a given point in time, that the future constitution finally reach this solidity which the teaching of repeated experiences would not fail to give it in everyone's mind."

The Revolution, in any case, will always risk falling back into the old rut, but as an event whose very content is unimportant, its existence attests to a permanent virtuality and cannot be forgotten. For future history, it is the guarantee of this continuity of an approach to progress.

I only wanted to situate this text by Kant on the *Aufklärung*. Further on, I will try to read it more closely. I also wanted to see how some fifteen years later, Kant was reflecting on this far more dramatic actuality of the French Revolution. With these two texts, we are in some way at the origins, at the starting point of a whole dynasty of philosophical questions. These two questions: "What is the *Aufklärung*?" and "What is Revolution?" are the two forms Kant used to ask the question about his own actuality. These are also, I believe, the two questions which kept haunting, if not all modern philosophy since the 19th century then at least the better part of that philosophy. After all, it very much seems to me that the *Aufklärung*, both as a singular event inaugurating European modernity and as the permanent process which manifests itself in the history of reason, in the development and the establishment of forms of rationality and techniques, the autonomy and the authority of knowledge, is not for us a mere episode in the history of ideas. It is a philosophical question, inscribed since the 18th century, in our thinking. Let us leave to their pious meditations those who want to keep the heritage of the *Aufklärung* alive and intact. This piety, of course, is the most touching of all treasons. Preserving the remains of the *Aufklärung* is not the issue, but rather it is the very question of this event and its meaning (the question of the historicity of the reflection on the universal) that must be maintained present and kept in mind as that which must be contemplated.

The question of the *Aufklärung*, or of reason, as a historical problem has in a more or less occult way traversed all philosophical thought from Kant until now. The flip side of the actuality that Kant encountered was the Revolution: the Revolution both as an event, as rupture and upheaval in history, as a failure, also as a value, as the sign of a pre-disposition that operates in history and in the progress of the human species. There again the question for philosophy is not to determine which is the part of the Revolution that it would be most fitting to preserve and uphold as a model. The question is to know what must be done with this will for revolution, with this *enthusiasm* for the Revolution which is something other than the revolutionary enterprise itself. The two questions: "What is the *Aufklärung*?" and "What to do with the will for revolution?" together define the field of philosophical questioning that is concerned with what we are in our present.

Kant seems to me to have founded the two great critical traditions which divide modern philosophy. Let us say that in his great critical work, Kant posited and founded this tradition of philosophy that asks the question of the conditions under which true knowledge is possible and we can therefore say that a whole side of modern philosophy since the 19th century has been defined and developed as the analytic of truth.

But there exists in modern and contemporary philosophy another type of question, another kind of critical questioning: it is precisely the one we see being born in the question of the *Aufklärung* or in the text on the Revolution. This other critical tradition poses the question: What is our actuality? What is the present field of possible experiences? It is not an issue of analyzing the truth, it will be a question rather of what we could call an ontology of ourselves, an ontology of the present. It seems to me that the philosophical choice with which we are confronted at present is this: we can opt for a critical philosophy which will present itself as an analytic philosophy of truth in general, or we can opt for a form of critical thought which will be an ontology of ourselves, an ontology of the actuality. It is this form of philosophy that, from Hegel to the Frankfurt School, through Nietzsche and Max Weber, has founded the form of reflection within which I have attempted to work.

Translated by Lysa Hochroth

3
What Is Enlightenment?

Today when a periodical asks its readers a question, it does so in order to collect opinions on some subject about which everyone already has an opinion; there is not much likelihood of learning anything new. In the eighteenth century, editors preferred to question the public on problems that did not yet have solutions. I don't know whether or not that practice was more effective; it was unquestionably more entertaining.

In any event, in line with this custom, in November 1784 a German periodical, *Berlinische Monatschrift*, published a response to the question: *Was ist Aufklärung?* And the respondent was Kant.

A minor text, perhaps. But it seems to me that it marks the discreet entrance into the history of thought of a question that modern philosophy has not been capable of answering, but that it has never managed to get rid of, either. And one that has been repeated in various forms for two centuries now. From Hegel through Nietzsche or Max Weber to Horkheimer or Habermas, hardly any philosophy has failed to confront this same question, directly or indirectly. What, then, is this event that is called the *Aufklärung* and that has determined, at least in part, what we are, what we think, and what we do today? Let us imagine that the *Berlinische Monatschrift* still exists and that it is asking its readers the question: What is modern philosophy? Perhaps we could respond with an echo: modern philosophy is the philosophy that is attempting to answer the question raised so imprudently two centuries ago: *Was ist Aufklärung?*

Let us linger a few moments over Kant's text. It merits attention for several reasons.

1. To this same question, Moses Mendelssohn had also replied in the same journal, just two months earlier. But Kant had not seen Mendelssohn's text when he wrote his. To be sure, the encounter of the German philosophical movement with the new development of Jewish culture does not date from this precise moment. Mendelssohn had been at that crossroads for thir-

ty years or so, in company with Lessing. But up to
this point it had been a matter of making a place
for Jewish culture within German thought—
which Lessing had tried to do in *Die Juden* or else
of identifying problems common to Jewish
thought and to German philosophy, this is what
Mendelssohn had done in his *Phadon oder, über die
Unsterblichkeit der Seele.* With the two texts published in the *Berlinische Monatschrift,* the German
Aufklärlung and the Jewish *Haskala* recognize that
they belong to the same history; they are seeking to
identify the common processes from which they
stem. And it is perhaps a way of announcing the
acceptance of a common destiny—we now know
to what drama that was to lead.

2. But there is more. In itself and within the
Christian tradition, Kant's text poses a new problem.

It was certainly not the first time that philosophical thought had sought to reflect on its own present.
But, speaking schematically, we may say that this
reflection had until then taken three main forms.

• The present may be represented as belonging
to a certain era of the world, distinct from the others through some inherent characteristics, or sepa-
rated from the others by some dramatic event.
Thus, in Plato's *The Statesman* the interlocutors

recognize that they belong to one of those revolutions of the world in which the world is turning backwards, with all the negative consequences that may ensue.

• The present may be interrogated in an attempt to decipher in it the heralding signs of a forthcoming event. Here we have the principle of a kind of historical hermeneutics of which Augustine might provide an example.

• The present may also be analyzed as a point of transition toward the dawning of a new world. That is what Vico describes in the last chapter of *La Scienza Nuova;* what he sees "today" is "a complete humanity...spread abroad through all nations, for a few great monarchs rule over this world of peoples"; it is also "Europe... radiant with such humanity that it abounds in all the good things that make for the happiness of human life."[1]

Now the way Kant poses the question of *Aufklärung* is entirely different: it is neither a world era to which one belongs, nor an event whose signs are perceived, nor the dawning of an accomplishment. Kant defines *Aufklärung* in an almost entirely negative way, as an *Ausgang,* an "exit," a "way out." In his other texts on history, Kant occasionally raises questions of origin or defines the internal teleology of a historical process. In the text on *Aufklärung,* he deals with the question of contemporary reality alone. He is not seeking to understand the present on the basis of a totality or of a future achievement. He is looking for a difference: What difference does today introduce with respect to yesterday?

3. I shall not go into detail here concerning this text, which is not always very clear despite its brevity. I should simply like to point out three or four features that seem to me important if we are to understand how Kant raised the philosophical question of the present day.

Kant indicates right away that the "way out" that characterizes Enlightenment is a process that releases us from the status of "immaturity." And by "immaturity," he means a certain state of our will that makes us accept someone else's authority to lead us in areas where the use of reason is called for. Kant gives three examples: we are in a state of "immaturity" when a book takes the place of our understanding, when a spiritual director takes the place of our conscience, when a doctor decides for us what our diet is to be. (Let us note in passing that the register of these three critiques is easy to recognize, even though the text does not make it explicit.) In any case, Enlightenment is defined by a modification of the preexisting relation linking will, authority, and the use of reason.

We must also note that this way out is presented by Kant in a rather ambiguous manner. He characterizes it as a phenomenon, an ongoing process; but he also presents it as a task and an obligation. From the very first paragraph, he notes that man himself is responsible for his immature status. Thus it has to be supposed that he will be able to escape from it only by a change that he himself will bring about in himself. Significantly, Kant says that this Enlightenment has a *Wahlspruch*: now a *Wahlspruch* is a heraldic device, that is, a distinctive feature by which one can be recognized, and it is also a motto, an instruction that one gives oneself and proposes to others. What, then, is this instruction? *Aude sapere*: "dare to know," "have the courage, the audacity, to know." Thus Enlightenment must be considered both as a process in which men participate collectively and as an act of courage to be accomplished personally. Men are at once elements and agents of a single process. They may be actors in the process to the extent that they participate in it; and the process occurs to the extent that men decide to be its voluntary actors.

A third difficulty appears here in Kant's text, in his use of the word "mankind," *Menschheit*. The importance of this word in the Kantian conception of history is well known. Are we to understand that the entire human race is caught up in the process of Enlightenment? In that case, we must imagine Enlightenment as a historical change that affects the political and social existence of all people on the face of the earth. Or are we to understand that it involves a change affecting what constitutes the humanity of human beings? But the question then arises of knowing what this change is. Here again, Kant's answer is not without a certain ambiguity. In any case, beneath its appearance of simplicity, it is rather complex.

Kant defines two essential conditions under which mankind can escape from its immaturity. And these two conditions are at once spiritual and institutional, ethical and political.

The first of these conditions is that the realm of obedience and the realm of the use of reason be clearly distinguished. Briefly characterizing the immature status, Kant invokes the familiar expression: "Don't think, just follow orders"; such is, according to him, the form in which military discipline, political power, and religious authority are usually exercised. Humanity will reach maturity when it is no longer required to obey, but when men are told: "Obey, and you will be able to reason as much as you like." We must note that the German word used here is *räsonieren;* this word, which is also used in the *Critiques,* does not refer to just any use of reason, but to a use of reason in which reason has no other end but itself: *räsonieren* is to reason for reasoning's sake. And Kant gives examples, these too being perfectly trivial in appearance: paying one's taxes, while being able to argue as much as one likes about the system of taxation, would be characteristic of the mature state; or again, taking responsibility for parish service, if one is a pastor, while reasoning freely about religious dogmas.

We might think that there is nothing very different here from what has been meant, since the sixteenth century, by freedom of conscience: the right to think as one pleases so long as one obeys as one must. Yet it is here that Kant brings into play another distinction, and in a rather surprising way. The distinction he introduces is between the private and public uses of reason. But he adds at once that reason must be free in its public use, and must be submissive in its private use. Which is, term for term, the opposite of what is ordinarily called freedom of conscience.

But we must be somewhat more precise. What constitutes, for Kant, this private use of reason? In what area is it exercised? Man, Kant says, makes a private use of reason when he is "a cog in a machine"; that is, when he has a role to play in society and jobs to do: to be a soldier, to have taxes to pay, to be in charge of a parish, to be a civil servant, all this makes the human being a particular segment of society; he finds himself thereby placed in a circumscribed position, where he has to apply particular rules and pursue particular ends. Kant does not ask that people practice a blind and foolish obedience, but that they adapt the use they make of their reason to these determined circumstances; and reason must then be subjected to the particular ends in view. Thus there cannot be, here, any free use of reason.

On the other hand, when one is reasoning only in order to use one's reason, when one is reasoning as a reasonable being (and not as a cog in a machine), when one is reasoning as a member of reasonable humanity, then the use of reason must be free and public. Enlightenment is thus not merely the process by which individuals would see their own personal freedom of thought guaranteed. There is Enlightenment when the universal, the free, and the public uses of reason are superimposed on one another.

Now this leads us to a fourth question that must be put to Kant's text. We can readily see how the

universal use of reason (apart from any private
end) is the business of the subject himself as an
individual; we can readily see, too, how the freedom of this use may be assured in a purely negative
manner through the absence of any challenge to it;
but how is a public use of that reason to be
assured? Enlightenment, as we see, must not be
conceived simply as a general process affecting all
humanity; it must not be conceived only as an
obligation prescribed to individuals: it now appears
as a political problem. The question, in any event,
is that of knowing how the use of reason can take
the public form that it requires, how the audacity to
know can be exercised in broad daylight, while
individuals are obeying as scrupulously as possible.
And Kant, in conclusion, proposes to Frederick II,
in scarcely veiled terms, a sort of contract—what
might be called the contract of rational despotism
with free reason: the public and free use of
autonomous reason will be the best guarantee of
obedience, on condition, however, that the political
principle that must be obeyed itself be in conformity with universal reason.

Let us leave Kant's text here. I do not by any
means propose to consider it as capable of constituting an adequate description of Enlightenment;
and no historian, I think, could be satisfied with it

for an analysis of the social, political, and cultural transformations that occurred at the end of the eighteenth century.

Nevertheless, notwithstanding its circumstantial nature, and without intending to give it an exaggerated place in Kant's work, I believe that it is necessary to stress the connection that exists between this brief article and the three *Critiques*. Kant in fact describes Enlightenment as the moment when humanity is going to put its own reason to use, without subjecting itself to any authority; now it is precisely at this moment that the critique is necessary, since its role is that of defining the conditions under which the use of reason is legitimate in order to determine what can be known, what must be done, and what may be hoped. Illegitimate uses of reason are what give rise to dogmatism and heteronomy, along with illusion; on the other hand, it is when the legitimate use of reason has been clearly defined in its principles that its autonomy can be assured. The critique is, in a sense, the handbook of reason that has grown up in Enlightenment; and, conversely, the Enlightenment is the age of the critique.

It is also necessary, I think, to underline the relation between this text of Kant's and the other texts he devoted to history. These latter, for the most part, seek to define the internal teleology of time and the point toward which history of humanity is moving. Now the analysis of Enlightenment, defining this history as humanity's passage to its adult status, situates contemporary reality with respect to the overall movement and its basic directions. But at the same time, it shows how, at this very moment, each individual is responsible in a certain way for that overall process.

The hypothesis I should like to propose is that this little text is located in a sense at the crossroads of critical reflection and reflection on history. It is a reflection by Kant on the contemporary status of his own enterprise. No doubt it is not the first time that a philosopher has given his reasons for undertaking his work at a particular moment. But it seems to me that it is the first time that a philosopher has connected in this way, closely and from the inside, the significance of his work with respect to knowledge, a reflection on history and a particular analysis of the specific moment at which he is writing and because of which he is writing. It is in the reflection on "today" as difference in history and as motive for a particular philosophical task that the novelty of this text appears to me to lie.

And, by looking at it in this way, it seems to me we may recognize a point of departure: the outline of what one might call the attitude of modernity.

I know that modernity is often spoken of as an epoch, or at least as a set of features characteristic of an epoch; situated on a calendar, it would be preceded by a more or less naive or archaic premodernity, and followed by an enigmatic and troubling "postmodernity." And then we find ourselves asking whether modernity constitutes the sequel to the Enlightenment and its development, or whether we are to see it as a rupture or a deviation with respect to the basic principles of the eighteenth century.

Thinking back on Kant's text, I wonder whether we may not envisage modernity rather as an attitude than as a period of history. And by "attitude," I mean a mode of relating to contemporary reality; a voluntary choice made by certain people; in the end, a way of thinking and feeling; a way, too, of acting and behaving that at one and the same time marks a relation of belonging and presents itself as a task. A bit, no doubt, like what the Greeks called an *ethos*. And consequently, rather than seeking to distinguish the "modern era" from the "premodern" or "postmodern," I think it would be more useful to try to find out how the attitude of modernity, ever since its formation, has found itself struggling with attitudes of "countermodernity."

To characterize briefly this attitude of modernity, I shall take an almost indispensable example, namely, Baudelaire; for his consciousness of modernity is widely recognized as one of the most acute in the nineteenth century.

1. Modernity is often characterized in terms of consciousness of the discontinuity of time: a break with tradition, a feeling of novelty, of vertigo in the face of the passing moment. And this is indeed what Baudelaire seems to be saying when he defines modernity as "the ephemeral, the fleeting, the contingent."[2] But, for him, being modern does not lie in recognizing and accepting this perpetual movement; on the contrary, it lies in adopting a certain attitude with respect to this movement; and this deliberate, difficult attitude consists in recapturing something eternal that is not beyond the present instant, nor behind it, but within it. Modernity is distinct from fashion, which does no more than call into question the course of time; modernity is the attitude that makes it possible to grasp the "heroic" aspect of the present moment. Modernity is not a phenomenon of sensitivity to the fleeting present; it is the will to "heroize" the present.

I shall restrict myself to what Baudelaire says about the painting of his contemporaries. Baudelaire makes fun of those painters who, finding nineteenth-century dress excessively ugly, want to depict nothing but ancient togas. But modernity in painting does not consist, for Baudelaire, in introducing black clothing onto the canvas. The modern painter is the one who can show the dark frock-coat as "the necessary costume of our time," the one who knows how to make manifest, in the fashion of the day, the essential, permanent, obsessive relation that our age entertains with death. "The dress-coat and frock-coat not only possess their political beauty, which is an expression of universal equality, but also their poetic beauty, which is an expression of the public soul—an immense cortege of undertaker's mutes (mutes in love, political mutes, bourgeois mutes...). We are each of us celebrating some funeral."[3] To designate this attitude of modernity, Baudelaire sometimes employs a litotes that is highly significant because it is presented in the form of a precept: "You have no right to despise the present."

2. This heroization is ironical, needless to say. The attitude of modernity does not treat the passing moment as sacred in order to try to maintain or perpetuate it. It certainly does not involve harvesting it as a fleeting and interesting curiosity. That would be what Baudelaire would call the specta-

tor's posture. The *flâneur*, the idle, strolling spectator, is satisfied to keep his eyes open, to pay attention and to build up a storehouse of memories. In
opposition to the *flâneur*, Baudelaire describes the
man of modernity: "Away he goes, hurrying,
searching.... Be very sure that this man... —this
solitary, gifted with an active imagination, cease-
lessly journeying across the great human desert —
has an aim loftier than that of a mere flaneur, an
aim more general, something other than the fugi-
tive pleasure of circumstance. He is looking for
that quality which you must allow me to call
'modernity.' ... He makes it his business to extract
from fashion whatever element it may contain of
poetry within history." As an example of modernity, Baudelaire cites the artist Constantin Guys. In
appearance a spectator, a collector of curiosities,
he remains "the last to linger wherever there can
be a glow of light, an echo of poetry, a quiver of life
or a chord of music; wherever a passion can *pose*
before him, wherever natural man and conven-
tional man display themselves in a strange beauty,
wherever the sun lights up the swift joys of the
depraved animal."[4]

But let us make no mistake. Constantin Guys is
not a *flâneur*; what makes him the modern painter
par excellence in Baudelaire's eyes is that, just when

the whole world is falling asleep, he begins to work, and he transfigures that world. His transfiguration does not entail an annulling of reality, but a difficult interplay between the truth of what is real and the exercise of freedom; "natural" things become "more than natural," "beautiful" things become "more than beautiful," and individual objects appear "endowed with an impulsive life like the soul of [their] creator."[5] For the attitude of modernity, the high value of the present is indissociable from a desperate eagerness to imagine it, to imagine it otherwise than it is, and to transform it not by destroying it but by grasping it in what it is. Baudelairean modernity is an exercise in which extreme attention to what is real is confronted with the practice of a liberty that simultaneously respects this reality and violates it.

3. However, modernity for Baudelaire is not simply a form of relationship to the present; it is also a mode of relationship that has to be established with oneself. The deliberate attitude of modernity is tied to an indispensable asceticism. To be modern is not to accept oneself as one is in the flux of the passing moments; it is to take oneself as object of a complex and difficult elaboration: what Baudelaire, in the vocabulary of his day,

calls *dandysme*. Here I shall not recall in detail the well-known passages on "vulgar, earthy, vile nature"; on man's indispensable revolt against himself; on the "doctrine of elegance" which imposes "upon its ambitious and humble disciples" a discipline more despotic than the most terrible religions; the pages, finally, on the asceticism of the dandy who makes of his body, his behavior, his feelings and passions, his very existence, a work of art. Modern man, for Baudelaire, is not the man who goes off to discover himself, his secrets and his hidden truth; he is the man who tries to invent himself. This modernity does not "liberate man in his own being"; it compels him to face the task of producing himself.

4. Let me add just one final word. This ironic heroization of the present, this transfiguring play of freedom with reality, this ascetic elaboration of the self—Baudelaire does not imagine that these have any place in society itself, or in the body politic. They can only be produced in another, a different place, which Baudelaire calls art.

I do not pretend to be summarizing in these few lines either the complex historical event that was the Enlightenment, at the end of the eighteenth century, or the attitude of modernity in the various guises it may have taken on during the last two centuries.

I have been seeking, on the one hand, to emphasize the extent to which a type of philosophical interrogation—one that simultaneously problematizes man's relation to the present, man's historical mode of being, and the constitution of the self as an autonomous subject—is rooted in the Enlightenment. On the other hand, I have been seeking to stress that the thread that may connect us with the Enlightenment is not faithfulness to doctrinal elements, but rather the permanent reactivation of an attitude—that is, of a philosophical ethos that could be described as a permanent critique of our historical era. I should like to characterize this ethos very briefly.

A. *Negatively*

1. This ethos implies, first, the refusal of what I like to call the "blackmail" of the Enlightenment. I think that the Enlightenment, as a set of political, economic, social, institutional, and cultural events on which we still depend in large part, constitutes a privileged domain for analysis. I also think that as an enterprise for linking the progress of truth

and the history of liberty in a bond of direct relation, it formulated a philosophical question that remains for us to consider. I think, finally, as I have tried to show with reference to Kant's text, that it defined a certain manner of philosophizing.

But that does not mean that one has to be "for" or "against" the Enlightenment. It even means precisely that one has to refuse everything that might present itself in the form of a simplistic and authoritarian alternative: you either accept the Enlightenment and remain within the tradition of its rationalism (this is considered a positive term by some and used by others, on the contrary, as a reproach); or else you criticize the Enlightenment and then try to escape from its principles of rationality (which may be seen once again as good or bad). And we do not break free of this blackmail by introducing "dialectical" nuances while seeking to determine what good and bad elements there may have been in the Enlightenment.

We must try to proceed with the analysis of ourselves as beings who are historically determined, to a certain extent, by the Enlightenment. Such an analysis implies a series of historical inquiries that are as precise as possible; and these inquiries will not be oriented retrospectively toward the "essential kernel of rationality" that can be found in the

Enlightenment and that would have to be preserved in any event; they will be oriented toward the "contemporary limits of the necessary," that is, toward what is not or is no longer indispensable for the constitution of ourselves as autonomous subjects.

2. This permanent critique of ourselves has to avoid the always too facile confusions between humanism and Enlightenment.

We must never forget that the Enlightenment is an event, or a set of events and complex historical processes, that is located at a certain point in the development of European societies. As such, it includes elements of social transformation, types of political institution, forms of knowledge, projects of rationalization of knowledge and practices, technological mutations that are very difficult to sum up in a word, even if many of these phenomena remain important today. The one I have pointed out and that seems to me to have been at the basis of an entire form of philosophical reflection concerns only the mode of reflective relation to the present.

Humanism is something entirely different. It is a theme or, rather, a set of themes that have reappeared on several occasions, over time, in European societies; these themes, always tied to value judgments, have obviously varied greatly in

their content, as well as in the values they have
preserved. Furthermore, they have served as a
critical principle of differentiation. In the seventeenth century, there was a humanism that pre
sented itself as a critique of Christianity or of reli
gion in general; there was a Christian humanism
opposed to an ascetic and much more theocentric
humanism. In the nineteenth century, there was a
suspicious humanism, hostile and critical toward
science, and another that, to the contrary, placed
its hope in that same science. Marxism has been a
humanism; so have existentialism and personalism
there was a time when people supported the
humanistic values represented by Nationa
Socialism, and when the Stalinists themselves said
they were humanists.

From this, we must not conclude that every
thing that has ever been linked with humanism is
to be rejected, but that the humanistic thematic is
in itself too supple, too diverse, too inconsistent to
serve as an axis for reflection. And it is a fact that
at least since the seventeenth century, what is
called humanism has always been obliged to lean
on certain conceptions of man borrowed from reli
gion, science, or politics. Humanism serves to
color and to justify the conceptions of man to
which it is, after all, obliged to resort to.

Now, in this connection, I believe that this thematic, which so often recurs and which always depends on humanism, can be opposed by the principle of a critique and a permanent creation of ourselves in our autonomy: that is, a principle that is at the heart of the historical consciousness that the Enlightenment has of itself. From this standpoint, I am inclined to see Enlightenment and humanism in a state of tension rather than identity.

In any case, it seems to me dangerous to confuse them; and further, it seems historically inaccurate. If the question of man, of the human species, of the humanist, was important throughout the eighteenth century, this is very rarely, I believe, because the Enlightenment considered itself a humanism. It is worthwhile, too, to note that throughout the nineteenth century, the historiography of sixteenth-century humanism, which was so important for people like Saint-Beuve or Burckhardt, was always distinct from and sometimes explicitly opposed to the Enlightenment and the eighteenth century. The nineteenth century had a tendency to oppose the two, at least as much as to confuse them.

In any case, I think that, just as we must free ourselves from the intellectual blackmail of "being for or against the Enlightenment," we must escape from the historical and moral confusionism that mixes the theme of humanism with the question of the Enlightenment. An analysis of their complex relations in the course of the last two centuries would be a worthwhile project, an important one if we are to bring some measure of clarity to the consciousness that we have of ourselves and of our past.

B. Positively

Yet while taking these precautions into account, we must obviously give a more positive content to what may be a philosophical ethos consisting in a critique of what we are saying, thinking, and doing, through a historical ontology of ourselves.

1. This philosophical ethos may be characterized as a *limit-attitude*. We are not talking about a gesture of rejection. We have to move beyond the outside-inside alternative, we have to be at the frontiers. Criticism indeed consists of analyzing and reflecting upon limits. But if the Kantian question was that of knowing what limits knowledge has to renounce transgressing, it seems to me that the critical question today has to be turned back into a positive one: in what is given to us as universal, necessary, obligatory, what place is occupied by

whatever is singular, contingent, and the product of arbitrary constraints? The point, in brief, is to transform the critique conducted in the form of necessary limitation into a practical critique that takes the form of a possible transgression.

This entails an obvious consequence: that criticism is no longer going to be practiced in the search for formal structures with universal value, but rather as a historical investigation into the events that have led us to constitute ourselves and to recognize ourselves as subjects of what we are doing, thinking, saying. In that sense, this criticism is not transcendental, and its goal is not that of making a metaphysics possible: it is genealogical in its design and archaeological in its method. Archaeological — and not transcendental — in the sense that it will not seek to identify the universal structures of all knowledge or of all possible moral action, but will seek to treat the instances of discourse that articulate what we think, say, and do as so many historical events. And this critique will be genealogical in the sense that it will not deduce from the form of what we are what it is impossible for us to do and to know; but it will separate out, from the contingency that has made us what we are, the possibility of no longer being, doing, or thinking what we are, do, or think. It is not seeking to make possible a metaphysics that has finally become a science; it is seeking to give new impetus, as far and wide as possible, to the undefined work of freedom.

2. But if we are not to settle for the affirmation or the empty dream of freedom, it seems to me that this historico-critical attitude must also be an experimental one. I mean that this work done at the limits of ourselves must, on the one hand, open up a realm of historical inquiry and, on the other, put itself to the test of reality, of contemporary reality, both to grasp the points where change is possible and desirable, and to determine the precise form this change should take. This means that the historical ontology of ourselves must turn away from all projects that claim to be global or radical. In fact we know from experience that the claim to escape from the system of contemporary reality so as to produce the overall programs of another society, of another way of thinking, another culture, another vision of the world, has led only to the return of the most dangerous traditions.

I prefer the very specific transformations that have proved to be possible in the last twenty years in a number of areas that concern our ways of being and thinking, relations to authority, relations between the sexes, the way in which we perceive

insanity or illness; I prefer even these partial transformations that have been made in the correlation
of historical analysis and the practical attitude, to
the programs for a new man that the worst political systems have repeated throughout the 20th
century.

I shall thus characterize the philosophical
ethos appropriate to the critical ontology of ourselves as a historico-practical test of the limits that
we may go beyond, and thus as work carried out
by ourselves upon ourselves as free beings.

3. Still, the following objection would no doubt
be entirely legitimate: if we limit ourselves to this
type of always partial and local inquiry or test, do
we not run the risk of letting ourselves be determined by more general structures of which we
may well not be conscious, and over which we may
have no control?

To this, two responses. It is true that we have to
give up hope of ever acceding to a point of view
that could give us access to any complete and definitive knowledge of what may constitute our historical limits. And from this point of view the theoretical and practical experience that we have of our
limits and of the possibility of moving beyond them
is always limited and determined; thus we are

always in the position of beginning again.

But that does not mean that no work can be done except in disorder and contingency. The work in question has its generality, its systematicity, its homogeneity, and its stakes.

(a) Its Stakes

These are indicated by what might be called "the paradox of the relations of capacity and power." We know that the great promise or the great hope of the eighteenth century, or a part of the eighteenth century, lay in the simultaneous and proportional growth of individuals with respect to one another. And, moreover, we can see that throughout the entire history of Western societies (it is perhaps here that the root of their singular historical destiny is located—such a peculiar destiny, so different from the others in its trajectory and so universalizing, so dominant with respect to the others), the acquisition of capabilities and the struggle for freedom have constituted permanent elements. Now the relations between the growth of capabilities and the growth of autonomy are not as simple as the eighteenth century may have believed. And we have been able to see what forms of power relation were conveyed by various technologies (whether we are speaking of productions with economic aims, or institutions whose goal is social regulation, or of techniques of communication): disciplines, both collective and individual, procedures of normalization exercised in the name of the power of the state, demands of society or of population zones, are examples. What is at stake, then, is this: How can the growth of capabilities be disconnected from the intensification of power relations?

(b) *Homogeneity*

This leads to the study of what could be called "practical systems." Here we are taking as a homogeneous domain of reference not the representations that men give of themselves, not the conditions that determine them without their knowledge, but rather what they do and the way they do it. That is, the forms of rationality that organize their ways of doing things (this might be called the technological aspect) and the freedom with which they act within these practical systems, reacting to what others do, modifying the rules of the game, up to a certain point (this might be called the strategic side of these practices). The homogeneity of these historico-critical analyses is thus ensured by this realm of practices, with their technological side and their strategic side.

(c) Systematicity

These practical systems stem from three broad areas: relations of control over things, relations of action upon others, relations with oneself. This does not mean that each of these three areas is completely foreign to the others. It is well known that control over things is mediated by relations with others; and relations with others in turn always entail relations with oneself, and vice versa. But we have three axes whose specificity and whose interconnections have to be analyzed: the axis of knowledge, the axis of power, the axis of ethics. In other terms, the historical ontology of ourselves has to answer an open series of questions; it has to make an indefinite number of inquiries which may be multiplied and specified as much as we like, but which will all address the questions systematized as follows: How are we constituted as subjects of our own knowledge? How are we constituted as subjects who exercise or submit to power relations? How are we constituted as moral subjects of our own actions?

(∂) Generality

Finally, these historico-critical investigations are quite specific in the sense that they always bear upon a material, an epoch, a body of determined practices and discourses. And yet, at least at the level of the Western societies from which we derive, they have their generality, in the sense that they have continued to recur up to our time: for example, the problem of the relationship between sanity and insanity, or sickness and health, or crime and the law; the problem of the role of sexual relations; and so on.

But by evoking this generality, I do not mean to suggest that it has to be retraced in its metahistorical continuity over time, nor that its variations have to be pursued. What must be grasped is the extent to which what we know of it, the forms of power that are exercised in it, and the experience that we have in it of ourselves constitute nothing but determined historical figures, through a certain form of problematization that defines objects, rules of action, modes of relation to oneself. The study of [modes of] problematization (that is, of what is neither an anthropological constant nor a chronological variation) is thus the way to analyze questions of general import in their historically unique form.

A brief summary, to conclude and to come back to Kant.

I do not know whether we will ever reach mature adulthood. Many things in our experience convince us that the historical event of the Enlightenment did not make us mature adults, and we have not reached that stage yet. However, it seems to me that a meaning can be attributed to that critical interrogation on the present and on ourselves which Kant formulated by reflecting on the Enlightenment. It seems to me that Kant's reflection is even a way of philosophizing that has not been without its importance or effectiveness during the last two centuries. The critical ontology of ourselves has to be considered not, certainly, as a theory, a doctrine, nor even as a permanent body of knowledge that is accumulating; it has to be conceived as an attitude, an ethos, a philosophical life in which the critique of what we are is at one and the same time the historical analysis of the limits that are imposed on us and an experiment with the possibility of going beyond them.

This philosophical attitude has to be translated into the labor of diverse inquiries. These inquiries have their methodological coherence in the at once archaeological and genealogical study of practices envisaged simultaneously as a technological type of rationality and as strategic games of liberties; they have their theoretical coherence in the definition of the historically unique forms in which the generalities of our relations to things, to others, to ourselves, have been problematized. They have their practical coherence in the care brought to the process of putting historico-critical reflection to the test of concrete practices. I do not know whether it must be said today that the critical task still entails faith in Enlightenment; I continue to think that this task requires work on our limits, that is, a patient labor giving form to our impatience for liberty.

Translated by Catherine Porter

NOTES

1 Giambattista Vico, *The New Science of Giambattista Vico*, 3rd ed., (1744), abridged trans. T. G. Bergin and M. H. Fisch (Ithaca / London: Cornell University Press, 1970), pp. 370, 372.

2 Charles Baudelaire, *The Painter of Modern Life and Other Essays*, trans. Jonathan Mayne (London Phaidon, 1964), p. 13.

3 Charles Baudelaire, "On the Heroism of Modern Life," in *The Mirror of Art: Critical Studies by Charles Baudelaire,* trans. Jonathan Mayne (London: Phaidon, 1955), p. 127.

4 Baudelaire, *Painter,* pp. 12, 11.

5 Ibid., p. 12.

4
For an Ethics of Discomfort

I t was toward the end of the Enlightenment, in 1784, that a Berlin newspaper raised the following question to good minds: "What is the *Aufklärung*? What is the Enlightenment?" Kant answered, after Mendelssohn.[1]

I find the question even more remarkable than the responses. For the "Enlightenment," at the end of this 18th century, was not new. It was not an invention, not a revolution, not a party. It was something familiar and diffused which was in the process of happening and of going away. The Prussian newspaper was basically asking: "What just happened to us? What is this event that is nothing other than what we have just said, thought and done — nothing other than ourselves, nothing other than this something that we were and that we still are?"

Should this curious investigation be inscribed in the history of journalism or philosophy? I only know that there have not been many philosophies, since this point in time, that do not revolve around the question: "Who are we at present? What are, therefore, these very fragile times from which we cannot detach our identity and which will carry it along with them?" I think that this question is also the core of the journalist's profession. The concern about what is happening—would Jean Daniel say otherwise?—is not so much inhabited by the desire to know how something can happen, always and all over the place; but rather by the desire to guess what is hidden under this exact, floating, mysterious and absolutely simple word: "Today."

Jean Daniel wrote *The Era of Ruptures*[2] vertically with respect to his journalistic career—overhanging it and flat up against it. It's the opposite of the "Time that remains." For some people, the destiny of time is to flee and thought is meant to be arrested. Jean Daniel is one of those for whom time remains and thought moves—not because it always thinks new things, but because it never ceases to think about the same things differently. This is precisely what makes it live and breathe. A treatise on mobile thought.

Each person has his or her own way of changing or, what amounts to the same thing, of perceiving that everything is changing. In this regard, nothing is more arrogant than wanting to impose one's law on others. My way of no longer being the same is, by definition, the most singular part of what I am. God knows, police patrols of ideology are not lacking; one hears their whistles: right, left, here, move on, right away, not now.... The pressure of identity and the injunction to break things up are both similarly abusive.

The periods dominated by great pasts—wars, resistance movements, revolutions—rather demand fidelity. Today, we rather go for ruptures. I cannot help thinking that there is something of a smile in the title Jean Daniel chose for his book. What he tells us are rather imperceptible moments of change, displacements, slidings, cracks, turn-abouts, gaps that increase, decrease, paths that get far, cave in and suddenly turn back. In fifteen years, since the foundation of *Le Nouvel Observateur*, Jean Daniel has changed, things have changed around him, the news magazine has changed, his colleagues, his friends and his adversaries have changed as well. All of them and each one of them, and each one with regard to everyone else.

Political courage was necessary, the mastery of oneself and of one's language in order to plunge oneself into this general mobility. Not to yield to the temptation of saying that nothing has changed that much, despite appearances. In order not to say either that: that's what happened, that's the powerful undertow and the force that carried everything with it. And especially not to assume a posture nor set oneself as a fixed point: I knew it. I've always told you that...

The "day" that has just changed? The day of the Left. The Left: not a coalition of parties on the political chess board, but an adherence that many felt without being able or wanting to give it a very clear definition. A kind of "essential" Left, a mixture of certainties and duties: "Country more than concept," and that, paradoxically, Jean Daniel, more than anyone else, had contributed to bringing into existence.

In the period immediately after World War II, belonging to this Left was not an easy task. Piggybacked on the Resistance, dependent on the U.S.S.R. and the "socialist camp," finally, proprietary of a doctrine, the Communist Party thus exerted a triple legitimacy: one that was historical, political and theoretical. It "imposed its law" on everything claiming to be from the Left: subjecting them to its law or making them outlaws. It magnetized the political field, orienting the neighboring filings, imposing a direction upon it. Either one was for it or against it, ally or adversary.

Khruschev, Budapest: the political justifications dissipate. Destalinization, the "crisis of Marxism": the theoretical legitimation gets foggy. And the opposition to the War of Algeria forms an historical reference about which, unlike the Resistance, the Party was notoriously absent. Without any law on the Left: the Left was able to emerge.

And the question asked by courageous anti-Stalinists: "We know very well who we are, but how can we really exist?" could be turned around: "We exist; it is now time to know who we are." This is the question that was the birth pact of *Le Nouvel Observateur.* From this heartfelt belonging, it was a matter of forming, not a party, not even an opinion, but a kind of self-awareness. *L'Ere des ruptures* recounts how the work, the persistence in making a blurred conscience clear ended up dismantling the certainties that had given birth to it.

In fact, this search for an identity has been done in a very strange way. Jean Daniel is right to retrospectively be surprised and find them "not that obvious," all these procedures that might have, at one time, seemed to be the obvious way of doing things.

First surprise. One sought less and less to position oneself according to the great geodeisics of history: capitalism, the bourgeois class, imperialism, socialism, the proletariat. Bit by bit, people began to give up pushing the "logical" and "historical" consequences of choices to inadmissible and intolerable limits. The heroism of political identity had had its day. We ask what we are, gradually, addressing the problems we struggle with: how to be involved in things and participate in them without getting trapped in them. Experience with... rather than *engagement* in....

Second surprise. It was neither the Union of the Left nor the Common Program, nor the relinquishing of the dictatorship of the proletariat by the "party of the revolution" that developed consciousness on the Left. Rather it was a small corner of the Middle East. It was bombings and camps in an Indochina which was no longer French. It was the Third World with revolutionary movements that develop there and authoritarian States that form there, Palestine, the Arabs and Israel, the concentrationary U.S.S.R.—and Gaullism perhaps due to the decolonization it achieved in spite of all the blind prophets—all this is what shook up the Left.

Third surprise. At the end of all these experiences or all these dreams, there is neither unanimity nor reward. Hardly was a consensus formed (for example against the American presence in Vietnam), than it got undone. Worse: it became more and more difficult for each person to remain absolutely in agreement with oneself. Rare were those who could say without blinking: "It was exactly what I had wanted." Identities are defined by trajectories.

Fourth surprise. From these scattered experiences, seemingly made in the name of approximately shared ideals, according to analogous forms of organization and in a vocabulary that can be understood from one culture to another, no universal thought was formed. Are we witnessing a globalization of the economy? Certainly. A globalization of political calculations? Without a doubt. But a universalization of political consciousness — certainly not.

Jean Daniel recounts these surprises: his, others', one of his being to realize that others still let themselves be surprised, those of others who are surprised or become indignant that he no longer gets surprised. And, at the end of this subtle tale, he unveils what for him constitutes the great "obvious fact" structuring the whole consciousness of the Left until then. This is that history is dominated by Revolution. Many on the Left had rejected this idea. But it was on the condition of finding a replacement for it. And of being able to say: I am doing just as well, but more cleanly and more securely. And it was necessary that, from the third world where it had not happened, this revolution return to us in the raw form of pure violence in order to lose the deaf obviousness that always placed it ahead of history.

Such is, it seems to me, what is at stake in the book: thirty years of experiences lead us "to have trust in no revolution," even if one can "understand each revolt." So what effect can such a conclusion have for a people—and a Left—who only loved "the later and more distant revolution" so much undoubtedly because of a deep, immediate conservatism? For fear of complete paralysis, one must tear oneself away from conservatism as one renounces the empty shell of a universal revolution. And this with all the more urgency since society's very existence is threatened by this conservatism, that is to say, by the inertia inherent to its development.

To the Left's old question: "We exist, but who are we?" this question to which the Left owes its existence without ever having given a response, Jean Daniel's book proposes to substitute this other interrogation: "Those who understand that it is necessary to wrest oneself from conservatism in order to be able to, at the very least, exist, and in the long term, not be completely dead, what must they be, or rather, what must they do?"

Jean Daniel did not attempt to reintroduce these moments in time, which always happen in life, when what we were so sure about suddenly turns out to be a mistake. His whole book is a search for these more subtle, more secret, and also more decisive moments, when the certainties are lost. They are difficult to grasp, not only because they never are precisely dated, but because they are always over and done with long before one finally becomes aware of them.

Of course, with these changes, new experiences or abrupt turnarounds in the world order have a role. But not the essential one. A reflection on the certainties that get mixed up, *L'Ere des ruptures* shows two things very well. First, an obvious fact gets lost, not when it is replaced by another which is fresher or cleaner, but when one begins to detect the very conditions that made it obvious: the familiarities which served as its support, the obscurities upon which its clarity was based, and all these things that, coming from far away, carried it secretly and made it such that "it was obvious."

And then, the new fact is always a bit of an idea from the back of one's mind anyway. It allows one

to see once again that which one never really lost
from sight. It gives the strange impression that one
had always rather thought what one never completely said and already said in a thousand ways
what one never really truly thought. Read, in the
chapter called "The Land Promised to All," the
pages on Palestinian rights and the Israeli fact. All
the lighting changes that trigger events or the
unexpected reversal of circumstances that are
made there by heightened shadows and lights:
those of Blida and those of Algeria from the past.

Reading these pages, it is impossible not to
recall Merleau-Ponty's lesson and what for him
was the essential, philosophical task. Never con-
sent to be completely comfortable with your own
certainties. Never let them sleep, but never believe
either that a new fact will be enough to reverse
them. Never imagine that one can change them
like arbitrary axioms. Remember that, in order to
give them an indispensable mobility, one must see
far, but also close-up and right around oneself.
One must clearly feel that everything perceived is
only evident when surrounded by a familiar and
poorly known horizon, that each certitude is only
sure because of the support offered by unexplored
ground. The most fragile instant has roots. There

is here a whole ethics of tireless evidence that does not exclude a rigorous economy of the True and the False; but is not reduced to it, either.

Translated by Lysa Hochroth

NOTES

1 M. Mendelssohn, "Über die Frage: Was heisst Aufklären?," *Berlinische Monatsschrift*, IV, No. 3, September 1784, pp. 193–200. I. Kant, "Beantwortung der Frage: Was ist Aufklärung?" *Berlinische Monatsschrift*, IV, No. 6, December 1784, pp. 491–494.

2 [Jean Daniel, *L'Ere des ruptures* (Paris: Grasset, 1979). Jean Daniel is the General Editor of *Le Nouvel Observateur*, a Left-leaning French weekley paper. Ed.]

5
What Our Present Is

Q: It would be interesting to me if you would tell us how you made your way through a series of problematics, a series of issues. Why you got interested in the history of psychiatry, the history of medicine, in prisons and now in the history of sexuality. Why, today, you seem to be interested in the history of law. What has been your itinerary? What was the driving force of your reflection, if it is possible to answer such a question?

MF: You are asking me a difficult question. First because the driving line cannot be determined until one is at the end of the road, and then, you know, I absolutely do not consider myself either a writer or a prophet. I work, it is true, for the most part in response to a set of circumstances, outside requests, various situations. I have no intention whatsoever of laying down the law and it seems to me that if there is a certain coherence in what I do, it is perhaps linked to a situation in which we all find ourselves, far more than a basic intuition or a systematic thinking. This has been true since Kant asked the question *"Was ist Aufklärung?"* that is, what is our own actuality, what is happening around us, what is our present. It seems to me that philosophy acquired a new dimension here. Moreover, it opened up a certain task that philosophy had ignored or didn't know even existed beforehand, and that is to tell us who we are, what our present is, what that is, today. It is obviously a question which would have had no meaning for Descartes. It is a question which begins to mean something for Kant, when he wonders what the *Aufklärung* is; it is, in a sense, Nietzsche's question. I also think that among the different functions that philosophy can and must have, there is also this one, asking oneself about who we are today, in our present actuality. I will say that it is around this that I raise the question and in this respect that I am Nietzschean or Hegelian or Kantian, from that very angle.

Well, how did I come to raise this type of question? Briefly, one can say the following about the

history of our intellectual life in post-war Western
Europe: first, during the 1950s, we had access to a
perspective of analysis very deeply inspired by
phenomenology which was, in a sense, at that time,
the dominant philosophy. I say dominant without
any pejorative in the word, for one cannot say that
there was a dictatorship or despotism in this way
of thinking; but in Western Europe, particularly in
France, phenomenology was a general style of
analysis. A style of analysis that claimed to analyze
concrete things as one of its fundamental tasks. It
is quite certain that from this point of view, one
could have remained a bit dissatisfied in that the
kind of concrete phenomenology referred to was a
bit academic and university-oriented. You had
privileged objects of phenomenological description, lived experiences or the perception of a tree
through an office window...

I am a little harsh but the object field that phenomenology explored was somewhat predeter-
mined by an academic philosophical tradition that
was perhaps worth opening up.

Secondly, another important form of dominant
thought was clearly Marxism. Marxism referred to
a whole domain of historical analysis which, in a
way, it left untouched. Reading Marx's texts and
the analysis of Marx's concepts was an important

task, but the content of historical knowledge to which these concepts had to refer, for which they had to be operational, these historical domains were a bit neglected. In any case, Marxism, or concrete Marxist history, at least in France, was not highly developed.

Then there was a third current which was especially developed and this was the history of sciences, with people like Bachelard, Canguilhem, etc…and Cavaillès. The problem was to know the following: is there a historicity of reason and can one devise the history of truth.

If you like, I would say that I situated myself at the intersection of these different currents and different problems. In relation to phenomenology, rather than making a somewhat internal description of lived experience, shouldn't one, couldn't one instead analyze a number of collective and social experiences?

As Binswanger showed, it is important to describe the conscience of the insane. And after all, is there not a cultural and social structuring of the experience of madness? And shouldn't that be analyzed?

This led me to a historical problem which was that of knowing: if one wants to describe the social, collective composition of an experience such as that of madness, what is the social field, what is the group of institutions and practices that must be historically analyzed and for which Marxist analyses are a bit like poorly tailored clothing.

And, thirdly, through the analysis of historical, collective and social experiences, linked to precise historical contexts, how can one define the history of knowledge, the history of what we know and how new objects are able to enter a domain of knowledge and can then be presented as objects to be known. So, if you like, concretely, that raises the following questions: is there an experience of madness which is characteristic of a given society, or not? How was this experience of madness able to constitute itself? How did it manage to emerge? And, through this experience of madness, how was madness presented as an object of knowledge for a kind of medicine which identified itself as mental medicine? Through which historical transformation, which institutional modification, was the experience of madness constituted with both the subjective pole of the experience of madness and the objective pole of mental illness?

Here is, if not the itinerary, at least the starting point. And, to return to the question you asked: why having chosen those objects? I will say that it seemed to me — and that was perhaps the fourth current, the fourth point of reference of my approach or of my attempts — that more literary texts existed, which were less integrated in a philosophical tradition. I am thinking about writers like Blanchot, Artaud, Bataille, who were very important for people of my generation. At bottom, they posed the problem of experiences on the edge, these forms of experiences that instead of being considered central, of being positively valued in a society, are deemed to be borderline experiences which put into question what is usually considered acceptable. Proceeding, in a sense, from the history of madness to a questioning of our system of reason.

Q: Madness as a borderline experience…

MF: That's it. For example, what is the relationship between medical thought, knowledge about illness and life? What is it in relation to the experience of death and how has the problem of death been integrated into this knowledge? Or how has this knowledge been indexed at this point in time, this absolute point of death? Same thing for crime in relation to the law. You interrogate the law itself, and what is the foundation of the law: taking crime as the point of rupture in relation to the system and adopting this point of view to raise the question: "Then what is the law?" Taking the prison as that which should enlighten us about what the penal system is, rather than taking the penal system for granted, interrogate it first from within, find out how it came about, how it was established and justified and only then, deduce what it was.

Q: You have presented contemporary philosophy in its actuality since Kant by asking a question which, basically, I think, interests us all and allows humans to question themselves about their position in history, in the world, in society. It seems to me that throughout all you have written from *Madness and Civilization* to *The History of Sexuality*, there is a perception of this reality that seems to especially concern you and which relates to everything one could call the techniques of containment, surveillance, control, in short, the way in which an individual in our society has been progressively controlled. Do you think that it is truly a question there of a classical element in our history, something essential to an understanding of modernity?

MF: Yes, it's true. It is not, if you like, a problem I wondered about in the beginning. While studying a number of things, namely, psychiatry, medicine, the penal system, little by little all these mechanisms of containment, exclusion, surveillance and individual control appeared to be very interesting, very important. I will say that I started raising these questions in a somewhat crude fashion when I realized that they were important ones. I believe that it is necessary to define what it is about and what kind of problem one can ask about all this. It seems to me that in most analyses, either properly philosophical or more political, if not with Marxist analyses, the question of power had been relatively marginalized or, in any case, simplified. Either it was a question of knowing the juridical bases which could legitimize a political power, or of defining power as a function of a simple conservation-reproduction in the relations of production. Then it was a matter of dealing with the philosophical question of the foundation of historical analysis of the superstructure. To me, this seemed insufficient or more exactly it was insufficient for a number of reasons. First because I believe—and many things in the concrete domains I have tried to analyze confirm it—that relations of power are much more deeply implanted than at the simple level of superstructures. Secondly, the question of the foundations of power is important but, forgive me, power isn't dependent on its foundation. There are powers which are unfounded but function very well and powers which tried to establish themselves, which actually managed to do so and which finally have no function. Therefore, if you like, my problem was to tell myself: but can't one study the way in which power really functions? So when I say "power," it is absolutely not a question of locating an instance or a kind of power that would be there, visible or hidden, it doesn't matter, and which would spread its deleterious beams across the social body or which would fatally extend its network. It is not power for something that would be the power to throw a tighter and tighter net strangling society and the people under its administration. It is certainly not about all that. Power is relations; power is not a thing, it is a relationship between two individuals, a relationship which is such that one can direct the behaviour of another or determine the behaviour of another. Voluntarily determining it in terms of a number of objectives which are also one's own. In other words, when one sees what power is, it is the exercise of something that one could call *government* in a very wide sense of the term. One can govern a society, one can govern a group, a community, a family; one can govern a person. When I say "govern someone," it is simply in the sense that one can determine one's behaviour in terms of a strategy by resorting to a number of tactics. Therefore, if you like, it is *governmentality* in the wide sense of the term, as the group of relations of power and techniques which allow these relations of power to be exercised, that is what I studied. How the mentally ill were governed; how the problem of governing the sick (once again, I put the word to govern in quotation marks, giving it both a rich and wide meaning); how the patients were governed, what one did with them, what status they were given, where they were placed, in what type of treatment, what kind of surveillance, also acts of kindness, philanthropy, economic field, care to be given to the ill: it is all that, I think, that one must try to see. So it is certain that this governmentality did not end, from one perspective, it became even more strict with the passing of time. The powers in a political system like those that existed in the Middle Ages, these powers understood in the sense of government of some by others, these were, in the end, rather loose. The problem was to extract taxes, which was necessary, useful. What people did with respect to their daily behaviour was not very important for the exercise of political power. It was very important, doubtless, in the ecclesiastical clergy whose power was a political power.

It is true that the number of objects that become objects of governmentality reflected inside political frameworks, even liberal ones, has increased a great deal. But I still do not think that one should consider that this governmentality necessarily takes on the tone of containment, surveillance and control. Through a whole series of subtle fabulations, one often actually ends up directing the behaviour of people or of acting in such a way that others' behaviour can have no negative effect on us later. And this is the field of governmentality that I wanted to study.

Q: And to study this object or the different objects that you studied, you used an historical method. But really what everyone sees today, and moreover, what for the most part makes for the originality of your analyses, not from the point of view of content but from the methodological point of view, is that you have operated a sort of displacement in historical method. That is, it is no longer the history of science, no longer an epistemology, no longer the history of ideologies, it is not even the history of institutions; one has the impression that it is all that at once but that in order to think about what psychiatry does, for example, or what criminologists do today—since criminologists called you here today—or in order to think about institutions such as prisons, asylums, etc...., you had to profoundly transform the way in which one conceived of history.

Does, for example, the opposition between knowledge and science that appears in your work and mainly in a number of your more methodological writings, seem to you more important from the perspective of the kind of history you are proposing to us?

MF: Well, I think, really, that the type of history I do carries a number of marks or handicaps, if you will. First, the thing that I would like to say is that the question I start off with is: what are we and what are we today? What is this instant that is ours? Therefore, if you like, it is a history that starts off from this present day actuality. The second thing is that in trying to raise concrete problems, what concerned me was to choose a field containing a number of points that are particularly fragile or sensitive at the present time. I would hardly conceive of a properly speculative history without the field being determined by something happening right now. So, the entire concern is not, of course, to follow what is happening and keep up with what is called fashion. Thus, for example, once one has written ten books, ten very good books, for that matter, on death, one doesn't have to write an eleventh one. One is not going to write an eleventh one, using as a pretext that it's a present day issue. The game is to try to detect those things which have not yet been talked about, those things that, at the present time, introduce, show, give some more or less vague indications of the fragility of our system of thought, in our way of reflecting, in our practices. Around 1955 when I was working in psychiatric hospitals, there was a kind of latent crisis, one felt very clearly that something was peeling off about which little had been said to date. It was, however, being experienced rather intensely. The best proof that this was being felt is that next door, in England, without ever having had any relationship with each other, people like Laing and Cooper were battling the very same problems. It is therefore a history which always refers to an actuality. As for the problem of medicine, it is true that the problem of medical power — in any case of the institutional field within which medical knowledge operates — was a question that was beginning to be asked, and was in fact widely discussed in the 1960s and which did not enter the public arena until after 1968. It is therefore history of actuality in the process of taking shape.

Q: Yes, but in terms of this actuality, the manner in which you tell its story seems original to me. It seems to be regulated by the very object you are analyzing. It is because of these key problems of our society that you are led to re-do history in a specific way.

MF: Fine. So, in terms of the objectives I set forth in this history, people often judge what I have done to be a sort of complicated, rather excessive analysis which leads to this result that finally we are imprisoned in our own system. The chords which bind us are numerous and the knots history has tied around us are oh so difficult to untie. In fact, I do just the opposite when I studied something like madness or prisons... Take the example of the prison: when we were discussing the reform of the penal system, a few years ago, say in the beginning of the 1970s, one thing that struck me in particular was that we could ask the theoretical question about the right to administer punishment or, on the other hand, we could deal with the problem of the re-organization of the penitentiary regime; but the kind of obvious fact that

depriving people of their liberty is really the sim-
plest, most logical, most reasonable, most equitable
form of punishing someone for an infraction of the
law, this was not very much discussed. So what I
wanted to do was to show how much finally this
equivalence—which for us is clear and simple—
between punishment and depriving people of their
liberty is in reality something relatively recent. It's
a technical invention whose origins are distant but
which was truly integrated into the penal system
and became part of penal rationality by the end of
the 18th century. And I have since then tried to
find out the reasons why the prison then became a
sort of obvious part of our penal system. It is a
matter of making things more fragile through this
historical analysis, or rather of showing both why
and how things were able to establish themselves
as such, and showing at the same time that they
were established through a precise history. It is
therefore necessary to place strategic logic inside
the things from whence they were produced, to
show that nonetheless, these are only strategies
and therefore, by changing a certain number of
things, by changing strategies, taking things differently, finally what appears obvious to us is not at
all so obvious. Our relationship to madness is an
historically established relationship, and from the

second that it is historically constituted, it can be politically destroyed. I say politically in the very wide sense of the term, in any case, there are possibilities for action because it is through many actions, reactions, etc... through many battles, many conflicts to respond to a certain number of problems, that specific solutions are chosen. I wanted to reintegrate a lot of obvious facts of our practices in the historicity of some of these practices and thereby rob them of their evidentiary status, in order to give them back the mobility that they had and that they should always have.

Q: Yes, in one of your present lectures, you use the term "veridiction" which refers to telling the truth and which touches on the problem of truth in the method. In what you just said concerning both your interest in actuality and the manner in which you envision history and its very constitution at the heart of this actuality, you question what one might consider the bases of one practice or another. About power, you said that power does not really function from its basis but that there are always justifications or philosophical reflections that aim at founding power. Your historical method, which is a method which performs a kind of archeology or genealogy according to the objects or the very development of your thought, aims at showing that finally, there are no bases for the practices of power. Would you agree in saying that from the philosophical perspective and in the entirety of your development, that what you aim at is also deconstructing any enterprise which would aim at giving power a basis?

MF: But I think that the activity of giving a basis to power is an activity that is made up of investigating what founds the powers I use or what can found the power that is used over me. I think that this question is important, essential. I would even say that this is the fundamental question. But the basis one gives in response to this question is part of the historical field within which it has a very relative place, that is to say, one does not find the foundation. It is very important that in a culture such as ours—as to whether or not one can find it in another culture I have no idea—since not only for centuries but for millenia, a number of things, like the exercise of political power, interrogate themselves or are interrogated by people who ask the question: but what are they doing?...There is critical work there.

Q: But what you find important is precisely the critical work of this question that keeps coming back.

MF: The basis of political power has been investigated for the last two millenia. When I say two millenia, I mean two millenia and a half. And it is this interrogation which is fundamental.

Q: And really the type of history you have done is very much an analysis of strategies, but also an analysis of the way in which a number of practices sought out their own basis.

MF: Absolutely. I am going to use a barbarous word but words are only barbarous when they do not clearly say what they mean; it is known that many familiar words are barbarous because they say many things at once or say nothing at all, but, on the other hand, certain technical words which are bizarre in their construction are not barbarous because they say fairly clearly what they mean. I will say that it's the history of *problematizations*, that is, the history of the way in which things become a problem. How, why and in what exact way, does madness become a problem in the modern world, and why has it become an important one? It is such an important problem that a number of things, for example, psychoanalysis (and God knows how much it is spread throughout our entire culture), take off from a problem which is absolutely contained within the relationships that one could have with madness. No, you know, it's the history of these problems. In what new way did illness become a problem; illness which was obviously always a problem. But, it seems to me, that there is a new way of problematizing illness starting with the 18th and 19th centuries.

So, it is not, in fact, the history of theories or the history of ideologies or even the history of mentalities that interests me, but the history of problems, moreover, if you like, it is the genealogy of problems that concerns me. Why a problem and why such a kind of problem, why a certain way of problematizing appears at a given point in time. For example, in the area of sexuality, it took me a very long time to perceive how one could answer that one: what the new problem was. You see, in terms of sexuality, it is not enough to indefinitely repeat the question: was it Christianity or was it industrialization that led to sexual repression? Repression of sexuality is only interesting where on one hand, it makes many people suffer, even today, and on the other hand, it has always taken on different forms but has always existed. What seems to me to be an important element to elucidate is how and why this relationship to sexuality, or this relationship with our sexual behaviours became a problem and what forms of it became a problem since it was always a problem. But it is certain that it was not the same kind of problem for the Greeks in the 4th century B.C. as it was for the Christians in the 3rd and 4th centuries, or in the 16th, 17th, etc...You know, this history of problematizations in human practices, there is a point where in some way the certainties all mix together, the lights go out, night falls, people begin to realize that they act blindly and that consequently a new light is necessary, new lighting and new rules of behaviour are needed. So, there it is, an object appears, an object that appears as a problem, *voilà*...

Q: I would like to ask you one last question. You were invited here by the Law School and you are now particularly interested in law and the juridical phenomenon. Can you briefly explain where this interest comes from and what you hope to get out of it?

MF: Listen, I have always been interested in the law, as a "layman"; I am not a specialist in rights, I am not a lawyer or jurist. But just as with madness, crime and prisons, I encountered the problem of rights, the law and the question that I always asked was how the technology or technologies of government, how these relations of power understood in the sense we discussed before, how all this could take shape within a society that pretends to function according to law and which, partly at least, functions by the law. So, these are connections, relationships of cause and effect, conflicts, too, and oppositions, irreductibilities between this functioning of the law and this technology of power, that is what I would like to study. It seems to me that it can be of interest to investigate juridical institutions, the discourse and practice of law from these technologies of power — not at all in the sense that this would totally shake up history and the theory of law, but rather that this could illuminate some rather important aspects of judicial practices and theories. Thus, to interrogate the modern penal system starting with corrective practices, starting with all these technologies that had to be modeled, modified, etc...the criminal individual, it seems to me that this allows many things to appear clearly. Therefore, if you like, I never stop getting into the issue of law and rights without taking it as a particular object. And if God grants me life, after madness, illness, crime, sexuality, the last thing that I would like to study would be the problem of war and the institution of war in what one could call the military dimension of society. There again I would have to cross into the problem of law, the rights of people and international law, etc...as well as the question of military justice: what makes a Nation entitled to ask someone to die for it.

Q: Indeed we hope that God will grant you life, so that we can read your histories, these multiple histories that have so enriched us. I thank you.

II
ABOUT THE BEGINNING OF THE HERMENEUTICS OF THE SELF

1
Subjectivity and Truth

In a work dealing with the moral treatment of madness and published in 1840, a French psychiatrist, Leuret, tells of the manner in which he has treated one of his patients—treated and, as you can imagine, of course, cured. One morning Dr. Leuret takes Mr. A., his patient, into a shower room. He makes him recount in detail his delirium.

"Well, all that," the doctor says, "is nothing but madness. Promise me not to believe in it anymore."

The patient hesitates, then promises.

"That's not enough," the doctor replies. "You have already made similar promises, and you haven't kept them." And the doctor turns on a cold shower above the patient's head.

"Yes, yes! I am mad!" the patient cries.

The shower is turned off, and the interrogation is resumed.

"Yes, I recognize that I am mad," the patient repeats, adding, "I recognize it, because you are forcing me to do so."

Another shower. Another confession. The interrogation is taken up again.

"I assure you, however," says the patient, "that I have heard voices and seen enemies around me."

Another shower.

"Well," says Mr. A., the patient, "I admit it. I am mad; all that was madness."[1]

To make someone suffering from mental illness recognize that he is mad is a very ancient procedure. Everybody in the old medicine, before the middle of the 19th century, everybody was convinced of the incompatibility between madness and recognition of madness. And in the works, for instance, of the 17th and of the 18th centuries, one finds many examples of what one might call truth-therapies. The mad would be cured if one managed to show them that their delirium is without any relation to reality.

But, as you see, the technique used by Leuret is altogether different. He is not trying to persuade his patient that his ideas are false or unreasonable. What happens in the head of Mr. A. is a matter of indifference for the doctor. Leuret wishes to obtain a precise act: the explicit affirmation, "I am mad." It is easy to recognize here the transposition within psychiatric therapy of procedures which have been used for a long time in judicial and religious institutions. To declare aloud and intelligibly the truth about one-self—I mean, to confess—has been considered for a long time in the Western world either a condition for redemption for one's sins or an essential item in the condemnation of the guilty. The bizarre therapy of Leuret may be read as an episode in the progressive culpabilization of madness. But, I would wish, rather, to take it as a point of departure for a more general reflection on this practice of confession, and on the postulate, which is generally accepted in Western societies, that one needs for his own salvation to know as exactly as possible who he is and also, which is something rather different, that he needs to tell it as explicitly as possible to some other people. The anecdote of Leuret is here only as an example of the strange and complex relationships developed in our societies between individuality, discourse, truth, and coercion.

In order to justify the attention I am giving to what is seemingly so specialized a subject, let me take a step back for a moment. All that, after all, is only for me a means that I will use to take on a much more general theme — that is, the genealogy of the modern subject.

In the years that preceded WWII, and even more so after WWII, philosophy in France and, I think, in all continental Europe, was dominated by the philosophy of the subject. I mean that philosophy set as its task *par excellence* the foundation of all knowledge and the principle of all signification as stemming from the meaningful subject. The importance given to this question of the meaningful subject was, of course, due to the impact of Husserl — only his *Cartesian Meditations* and the *Crisis* were generally known in France[2] — but the centrality of the subject was also tied to an institutional context. For the French university, since philosophy began with Descartes, it could only advance in a Cartesian manner. But we must also take into account the political conjuncture. Given the absurdity of wars, slaughters, and despotism, it seemed then to be up to the individual subject to give meaning to his existential choices.

With the leisure and distance that came after the war, this emphasis on the philosophical subject no longer seemed so self-evident. Two hitherto-hidden theoretical paradoxes could no longer be avoided. The first one was that the philosophy of consciousness had failed to found a philosophy of knowledge, and especially scientific knowledge, and the second was that this philosophy of meaning paradoxically had failed to take into account the formative mechanisms of signification and the structure of systems of meaning. I am aware that another form of thought claimed then to have gone beyond the philosophy of the subject—this, of course, was Marxism. It goes without saying—and it goes indeed better if we say it—that neither materialism nor the theory of ideologies successfully constituted a theory of objectivity or of signification. Marxism put itself forward as a humanistic discourse that could replace the abstract subject with an appeal to the real man, to the concrete man. It should have been clear at the time that Marxism carried with it a fundamental theoretical and practical weakness: the humanistic discourse hid the political reality that the Marxists of this period nonetheless supported.

With the all-too-easy clarity of hindsight—what you call, I think, the "Monday morning quarterback"—let me say that there were two possible paths that led beyond this philosophy of the subject. First, the theory of objective knowledge and, two, an analysis of systems of meaning, or semiology. The first of these was the path of logical positivism. The second was that of a certain school of linguistics, psychoanalysis, and anthropology, all generally grouped under the rubric of structuralism.

These were not the directions I took. Let me announce once and for all that I am not a structuralist, and I confess with the appropriate chagrin that I am not an analytic philosopher—nobody is perfect. I have tried to explore another direction. I have tried to get out from the philosophy of the subject through a genealogy of this subject, by studying the constitution of the subject across history which has led us up to the modern concept of the self. This has not always been an easy task, since most historians prefer a history of social processes [where society plays the role of subject] and most philosophers prefer a subject without history. This has neither prevented me from using the same material that certain social historians have used, nor from recognizing my theoretical debt to those philosophers who, like Nietzsche, have posed the question of the historicity of the subject. [So much for the general project. Now a few words on methodology. For this kind of research, the history of science constitutes a privileged point of view. This might seem paradoxical. After all, the genealogy of the self does not take place within a field of scientific knowledge, as if we were nothing else than that which rational knowledge could tell us about ourselves. While the history of science is without doubt an important testing ground for the theory of knowledge, as well as for the analysis of meaningful systems, it is also fertile ground for studying the genealogy of the subject. There are two reasons for this. All the practices by which the subject is defined and transformed are accompanied by the formation of certain types of knowledge, and in the West, for a variety or reasons, knowledge tends to be organized around forms and norms that are more or less scientific. There is also another reason, maybe more fundamental and more specific to our societies. I mean the fact that one of the main moral obligations for any subject is to know oneself, to tell the truth about oneself, and to constitute oneself as an object of knowledge both for other people and for oneself. The truth obligation for individuals and a scientific organization of knowledge; those are the two reasons why the history of knowledge constitutes a privileged point of view for the genealogy or the subject.

Hence, it follows that I am not trying to do history of sciences in general, but only of those which sought to construct a scientific knowledge of the subject. Another consequence. I am not trying to measure the objective value of these sciences, nor to know if they can become universally valid. That is the task of an epistemological historian. Rather, I am working on a history of science that is, to some extent, regressive history seeking to discover the discursive, the institutional and the social practices from which these sciences arose. This would be an archaeological history. Finally, the third consequence, this project seeks to discover the point at which these practices became coherent reflective techniques with definite goals, the point at which a particular discourse emerged from those techniques and came to be seen as true, the point at which they are linked with the obligation of searching for the truth and telling the truth. In sum, the aim of my project is to construct a genealogy of the subject. The method is an archaeology of knowledge, and the precise domain of the analysis is what I should call technologies. I mean the articulation of certain techniques and certain kinds of discourse about the subject.

I would like to add one final word about the practical significance of this form of analysis. For Heidegger, it was through an increasing obsession with *techné* as the only way to arrive at an understanding of objects, that the West lost touch with Being. Let's turn the question around and ask which techniques and practices constitute the Western concept of the subject, giving it its characteristic split of truth and error, freedom and constraint. I think that it is here that we will find the real possibility of constructing a history of what we have done and, at the same time, a diagnosis of what we are. At the same time, this theoretical analysis would have a political dimension. By this phrase 'political dimension' I mean an analysis that relates to what we are willing to accept in our world, to accept, to refuse, and to change, both in ourselves and in our circumstances. In sum, it is a question of searching for another kind of critical philosophy. Not a critical philosophy that seeks to determine the conditions and the limits of our possible knowledge of the object, but a critical philosophy that seeks the conditions and the indefinite possibilities of transforming the subject, of transforming ourselves.]

Up to the present I have proceeded with this general project in two ways. I have dealt with the modern theoretical constitutions that were concerned with the subject in general. I have tried to analyze in a previous book theories of the subject as a speaking, living, working being.[3] I have also dealt with the more practical understanding produced in those institutions like hospitals, asylums, and prisons, where certain subjects became objects of knowledge and at the same time objects of domination.[4] And now, I wish to study those forms of understanding which the subject creates about himself. Those forms of self-understanding are important, I think, to analyze the modern experience of sexuality.[5]

But since I have started with this last type of project I had to change my mind on several important points. Let me introduce a kind of autocritique. According to some suggestions by Habermas, it seems, one can identify three major types of techniques in human societies: the techniques which allow one to produce, to transform, to manipulate things; the techniques which allow one to use sign systems; and the techniques which allow one to determine the behavior of individuals, to impose certain wills on them, and to submit them to certain ends or objectives. That is to say, there are techniques of production, techniques of signification, and techniques of domination.[6]

Of course, if one wants to study the history of natural sciences, it is useful, if not necessary, to take into account techniques of production and semiotic techniques. But since my project was concerned with the knowledge of the subject, I thought that the techniques of domination were the most important, without any exclusion of the rest. But, analyzing the experience of sexuality, I became more and more aware that there is in all societies, I think, in all societies whatever they are, another type of techniques: techniques which permit individuals to perform, by their own means, a certain number of operations on their own bodies, on their own souls, on their own thoughts, on their own conduct, and this in such a way that they transform themselves, modify themselves, and reach a certain state of perfection, of happiness, of purity, of supernatural power, and so on. Let's call this kind of techniques a techniques or technology of the self.[7]

I think that if one wants to analyze the genealogy of the subject in Western civilization, he has to take into account not only techniques of domination but also techniques of the self. Let's say: he has to take into account the interaction between those two types of techniques—techniques of domination and techniques of the self. He has to take into account the points where the technologies of domination of individuals over one another overlap processes by which the individual acts upon himself. And conversely, he has to take into account the points where the techniques of the self are integrated into structures of coercion or domination. The contact point, where the individuals are driven [and known] by others is tied to the way they conduct themselves [and know themselves]. It is what we can call, I think, government.[8] Governing people, in the broad meaning of the word [as they spoke of it in the 16th century, of governing children, or governing family, or governing souls] is not a way to force people to do what the governor wants; it is always a versatile equilibrium, with complementarity and conflicts between techniques which impose coercion and processes through which the self is constructed or modified by himself.

When I was studying asylums, prisons, and so on, I insisted, I think, too much on the techniques of domination. What we can call discipline is something really important in these kinds of institutions, but it is only one aspect of the art of governing people in our society. We should not understand the exercise of power as pure violence or strict coercion. Power consists in complex relations: these relations involve a set of rational techniques, and the efficiency of those techniques is due to a subtle integration of coercion-technologies and self-technologies. I think that we have to get rid of the more or less Freudian schema—you know it—the schema of interiorization of the law by the self. Fortunately, from a theoretical point of view, and maybe unfortunately from a practical point of view, things are much more complicated. In short, having studied the field of government by taking as my point of departure techniques of domination, I

would like in years to come to study government—
especially in the field of sexuality—starting from
the techniques of the self.[9]

Among those techniques of the self in this field of
the self-technology, I think that the techniques
directed toward the discovery and the formulation
of the truth concerning oneself are extremely
important; and if, for the government of people in
our societies, everyone had not only to obey but also
to produce and publish the truth about oneself, then
examination of conscience and confession are
among the most important of those procedures. Of
course, there is a very long and very complex history, from the Delphic precept, *gnothi seauton* ("know
yourself") to the strange therapeutics promoted by
Leuret, which I was describing in the beginning of
this lecture. There is a very long way from one to
the other, and I don't want, of course, to give you
even a survey this evening. I'd like only to emphasize a transformation of those practices, a transformation which took place at the beginning of the
Christian era, of the Christian period, when the
ancient obligation of knowing oneself became the
monastic precept "confess, to your spiritual guide,
each of your thoughts." This transformation is, I
think, of some importance in the genealogy of modern subjectivity. With this transformation starts

what we would call the hermeneutics of the self. This evening I'll try to outline the way confession and self-examination were conceived by pagan philosophers, and next week I'll try to show you what it became in early Christianity.

It is well known that the main objective of the Greek schools of philosophy did not consist of the elaboration, the teaching, of theory. The goal of the Greek schools of philosophy was the transformation of the individual. The goal of Greek philosophy was to give the individual the quality which would permit him to live differently, better, more happily, than other people. What place did self-examination and confession have in this? At first glance, in all the ancient philosophical practices, the obligation to tell the truth about oneself occupies a rather limited place. And this for two reasons, both of which remain valid throughout the whole Greek and Hellenistic Antiquity. The first of those reasons is that the objective of philosophical training was to equip the individual with a number of precepts which permit him to conduct himself in all circumstances of life without losing mastery of himself or without losing tranquility of spirit, purity of body and soul. From this principle stems the importance of the master's discourse. The master's discourse has to talk, to explain, to persuade; he has to give the disciple a universal code for all his life, so that the verbalization takes place on the side of the master and not on the side of the disciple.

There is also another reason why the obligation to confess does not have a lot of importance in the direction of the classical conscience. The tie with the master then was circumstantial or, in any case, provisional. It was a relationship between two wills, which does not imply a complete or a definitive obedience. One solicits or one accepts the advice of a master or of a friend in order to endure an ordeal, a bereavement, an exile, or a reversal of fortune, and so on. Or again, one places oneself under the direction of a master for a certain period of one's life so as to be able one day to behave autonomously and no longer have need of advice. Ancient direction tends toward the autonomy of the directed. Under these conditions, one can understand that the necessity for exploring oneself in exhaustive depth does not present itself. It is not indispensable to say everything about oneself, to reveal one's slightest secrets, so that the master may exert complete power over one. The exhaustive and continual presentation of oneself under the eyes of an all-powerful director is not an essential feature of this technique of direction.

But, despite this general orientation which puts so little emphasis on self-examination and on confession, one finds well before Christianity already elaborated techniques for discovering and formulating the truth about oneself. And their role, it would seem, became more and more important. The growing importance of these techniques is no doubt tied to the development of communal life in the philosophical school, as with the Pythagoreans or the Epicureans, and it is also tied to the value given to the medical model, either in the Epicurean or the Stoician schools.

Since it is not possible in so short a time even to give a sketch of this evolution of Greek and Hellenist civilization, I'll take only two passages of a Roman philosopher, Seneca. They may be considered rather good witnesses on the practice of self-examination and confession as it existed with the Stoics of the Imperial period at the time of the birth of Christianity. The first passage can be found in the *De Ira* of Seneca. Here is the passage I'll read it to you:

"What could be more beautiful than to conduct an inquest on one's day? What sleep better than that which follows this review of one's actions? How calm it is, deep and free, when the soul has received its portion of praise and blame, and has submitted itself to its own examination, to its own censure. Secretly, it makes the trial of its own conduct. I exercise this authority over myself, and each day I will myself as witness before myself. When my light is lowered and my wife at last is silent, I reason with myself and take the measure of my acts and of my words, I hide nothing from myself; I spare myself nothing. Why, in effect, should I fear anything at all from amongst my errors whilst I can say: 'Be vigilant in not beginning it again; today I will forgive you. In a certain discussion you spoke too aggressively or you did not correct the person you were reproaching, you offended him…' " etc.[10]

There is something paradoxical in seeing the Stoics, such as Seneca and also Sextus, Epictetus, Marcus Aurelius, and so on, giving so much importance to the examination of conscience whilst, according to the terms of their doctrine, all faults were supposed equal. It should not therefore be necessary to interrogate oneself on eachaccount.

But, let's look at this text a little more closely. First of all, Seneca uses a vocabulary which at first glance appears, above all, judicial. He uses expressions like *cognoscere de moribus suis*, and *me causam dico* — all that is typical judicial vocabulary. It seems, therefore, that the subject is, with regard to himself, both the judge and the accused. In this

examination of conscience it seems that the subject
divides itself in two and organizes a judicial scene,
where it plays both roles at once. Seneca is like a
defendant confessing his crime to the judge, and
the judge is Seneca himself. But, if we look more
closely, we see that the vocabulary used by Seneca
is much more administrative than judicial. It is the
vocabulary of the direction of goods or territory.
Seneca says, for instance, that he is *speculator sui,*
that he inspects himself, that he examines the past
day with himself, *totum diem meum scrutor;* or that he
takes the measure of things said and done; he uses
the word *remetior.* With regard to himself, he is not
a judge who has to punish; he is, rather, an admin-
istrator who, once the work has been done or the
year's business finished, does the accounts, takes
stock of things, and sees if everything has been
done correctly. Seneca is a permanent administra-
tor of himself, more than a judge of his own past.[11]

The kind of faults Seneca made and for which
he reproaches himself are significant from this
point of view. He reproaches himself for having
criticized someone and for hurting him instead of
correcting him; or again, he says that he has talked
to people who were, in any case, incapable of
understanding him. These faults, as he says himself, are not really faults; they are mistakes. And

why mistakes? Either because he did not keep in his mind the aims which the sage should set himself or because he had not correctly applied the rules of conduct to be deduced from them. The faults are mistakes in that they are bad adjustments between aims and means. Significant is also the fact that Seneca does not recall those faults in order to punish himself; his only goal is to memorize exactly the rules which he had to apply. This memorization is meant to reactivate fundamental philosophical principles and readjust their application. In the Christian confession the penitent has to memorize the law in order to discover his own sins, but in this Stoic exercise the sage memorizes acts in order to reactivate the fundamental rules.

One can therefore characterize this examination in a few words. First, the goal of this examination is not at all to discover the truth hidden in the subject, it is rather to recall the truth forgotten by the subject. Two, what the subject forgets is not himself, nor his nature, nor his origin, nor a supernatural affinity. What the subject forgets is what he ought to have done, that is, a collection of rules of conduct that he had learned. Three, the recollection of errors committed during the day serves to measure the distance which separates what has been done from what should have been done. And four, the subject who practices this examination on himself is not the operating ground for a process more or less obscure which has to be deciphered. He is the point where rules of conduct come together and register themselves in the form of memories. He is at the same time the point of departure for actions more or less in conformity with these rules. He constitutes — the subject constitutes — the point of intersection between a set of memories which must be brought into the present and acts which have to be regulated.

This evening's examination takes place logically among a set of other Stoic exercises [all of them being a way to incorporate in a constant attitude a code of actions and reactions, whatever situation may occur]: continual reading, for instance, of the manual of precepts (that's for the present); the examination of the evils which could happen in life, the well-known *premeditatio malorum* (that was for the possible); the enumeration each morning of the tasks to be accomplished during the day (that was for the future); and finally, the evening examination of conscience (so much for the past). As you see, the self in all those exercises is not considered as a field of subjective data which have to be interpreted. It submits itself to the trial of possible or real action.

Well, after this examination of conscience, which constitutes a kind of confession to one's self, I would like to speak about the confession to others: I mean to say the exposé of one's soul which one makes to someone, who may be a friend, an adviser, a guide. This was a practice not very developed in philosophical life, but it had been developed in some philosophical schools, for instance among the Epicurean schools, and it was also a very well known medical practice. The medical literature is rich in such examples of confession or exposé of the self. For instance, the treatise of Galen *On the Passions of the Soul*[12] quotes such an example; or Plutarch, in the *De Profectibus in Virtute* writes, "There are many sick people who accept medicine and others who refuse them; the man who hides the shame of soul, his desire, his unpleasantness, his avarice, his concupiscence, has little chance of making progress. Indeed, to speak one's evil reveals one['s] nastiness; to recognize it instead of taking pleasure in hiding it, all this is a sign of progress."[13]

Well, another text of Seneca might also serve us as an example here of what was confession in the Late Antiquity. It is in the beginning of *De Tranquillitate Animi*.[14] Serenus, a young friend of Seneca, comes to ask him for advice. It is very explicitly a medical consultation on the state of his

own soul. "Why," says Serenus, "should I not confess to you the truth, as to a doctor?... I do not feel
altogether ill but nor do I feel entirely in good
health." Serenus experiences a state of malaise, as it
were, he says, like on a boat which does not
advance, but is tossed about by the rolling of the
ship. And, he fears that he will stay at sea in this
condition, in view of the land and of the virtues
which remain inaccessible. In order to escape this
state, Serenus therefore decides to consult Seneca
and to confess what he feels to Seneca. He says that
he wants *verum fateri,* to tell the truth, to Seneca.
[But, through this confession, through this description of his own state, he asks Seneca to tell him the
truth about his own state. Seneca is at the same
time confessing the truth and lacking in truth.]

Now what is this truth, what is this *verum,* that
he wants to confess? Does he confess faults, secret
thoughts, shameful desires, and things of that sort?
Not at all. Serenus's text is made up of an accumu-
lation of relatively unimportant — at least for us
unimportant — details; for instance, Serenus confesses to Seneca that he uses the earthenware
inherited from his father, that he gets easily carried
away when he makes public speeches, and so on
and so on. But beneath the apparent disorder of
this confession it is easy to recognize three distinct

domains: the domain of riches, the domain of political life, and the domain of glory; to acquire riches, to participate in the affairs of the city, to gain public recognition. These are—these were—the three types of activity available to a free man, the three commonplace moral questions that are examined by the major philosophical schools of the period. The framework of Serenus's exposé is not therefore defined by the real course of his existence; it is not defined by his real experiences, nor by a theory of the soul or of its elements, but only by a classification of the different types of activity which one can exercise and the ends which one can pursue. In each one of these fields, Serenus reveals his attitude by enumerating what pleases him and what displeases him. The expression "it pleases me" *(placet me)* is the leading thread in his analysis. It pleases him to do favors for his friends. It pleases him to eat simply, and to only have what he has inherited, but the spectacle of luxury in others pleases him. He also takes pleasure in inflating his oratorical style in the hope that posterity will remember his words. In describing what pleases him, Serenus is not seeking to reveal what are his deepest desires. His pleasures are not a way of revealing what Christians will later call *concupiscentia*. For him, it is a question of his own state and of adding something to the knowledge of the moral precepts. This addition to what is already known is a force, the force capable of transforming pure knowledge and simple consciousness into a real way of living. And that is what Seneca tries to do when he uses a set of persuasive arguments, demonstrations, examples, in order not to discover a still unknown truth inside and deep into Serenus's soul but in order to explain, if I may say, to which extent truth in general is true. The objective of Seneca's discourse is not to add a force of coercion coming from elsewhere to some theoretical principle but to change them into a victorious force. Seneca has to give a place to truth as a force.

Hence, I think, several consequences. First, in this game between Serenus's confession and Seneca's consultation, truth, as you see, is not defined by a correspondence to reality but as a force inherent to principles and which has to be developed in a discourse. Two, this truth is not something which is hidden behind or under the consciousness in the deepest and most obscure part of the soul. It is something which is in front of the individual as a point of attraction, a kind of magnetic force which attracts him towards a goal. Three, this truth is not reached by an analytical exploration of what is supposed to be real in the

individual but by rhetorical explanation of what
is good for anyone who wants to reach the life of
a sage. Four, the confession is not directed
towards an individualization of Serenus through
the discovery of some personal characteristics but
towards the constitution of a self which could be
at the same time and without any discontinuity
subject of knowledge and subject of will. Five, [if
the role of confession and consultation is to give
place to truth as a force, it is easy to understand
that self-examination has nearly the same role. We
have seen that if every evening Seneca recalls his
mistakes, it is to memorize the moral precepts of
the conduct, and memory is nothing else than the
force of the truth when it is permanently present
and active in the soul. A permanent memory in the
individual and in his inner discourse, a persuasive
rhetorics in the master's advice—those are the
aspects of truth considered as a force. Then, we
may conclude, in ancient philosophy self-examination and confession may be considered truth-game,
and an important truth-game, but the objective of
this truth-game is not to discover a secret reality
inside the individual. The objective of this truth-
game is to turn the individual into a place where
truth can appear and act as a real force through the
presence of memory and the efficiency of dis-

course.] We can see that such a practice of confession and consultation remains within the framework of what the Greeks for a long time called the *gnomé*. The term *gnomé* designates the unity of will and knowledge; it also designates a brief piece of discourse through which truth may appear with all its force and encrust itself in the soul of people. [In the earliest form of Greek philosophy, poets and divine men told the truth to ordinary mortals through this kind of *gnomé*. *Gnomai* were very short, very imperative, and so deeply illuminated by the poetical light that it was impossible to forget them and to avoid their power. Well, I think you can see that self-examination, confession — as you find them, for instance, in Seneca, but also in Marcus Aurelius, Epictetus, and so on, even as late as the first century A.D. — self-examination and confession were still a kind of development of the *gnomé* .] Then, we could say that even as late as the first century A.D., the type of subject which is proposed as a model and as a target in the Greek, or in the Hellenistic or Roman, philosophy, is a gnomic self, where the force of truth is one with the form of the will.

In this model of the gnomic self, we found several constitutive elements: the necessity of telling the truth about oneself, the role of the master and the master's discourse, the long way that finally leads to the emergence of the self. All those elements we also find in the Christian technologies of the self, but with a very different organization. I should say, in sum, and I'll conclude there, that as far as we followed the practices of self-examination and confession in the Hellenistic or Roman philosophy, you see that the self is not something that has to be discovered or deciphered as a very obscure text. You see that the task is not to bring to light what would be the most obscure part of our selves. On the contrary, the self doesn't have to be discovered but to be constituted, to be constituted through the force of truth. This force lies in [the mnemonic aptitude of the individual and] the rhetorical quality of the master's discourse, and this rhetorical quality depends in part on the exposé of the disciple, who has to explain how far he is in his way of living from the true principles that he knows. [These depend in part on the arts of memory and the acts of persuasion. So, technologies of the self in the ancient world are not linked with an art of interpretation, but with arts such as mnemotechnics and rhetoric. Self-observation, self-interpretation, self-hermeneutics won't intervene in the technologies of the self before Christianity.] And I think that this organization of the self as a target, the organization of what I call the gnomic self, as the objective, the aim towards which the confession and the self-examination is directed, is something vastly different from what we meet in the Christian technologies of the self. In the Christian technologies of the self, the problem is to discover what is hidden inside the self; the self is like a text or like a book that we have to decipher, and not something which has to be constructed by the superposition, the superimposition of the will and the truth. This organization, this Christian organization, so different from the pagan one, is something which is, I think, quite decisive for the genealogy of the modern self, and that's the point I'll try to explain next week when we meet again. Thank you.

2
Christianity and Confession

The theme of this lecture is the same as the theme of last week's lecture. [Well, several persons asked me to give a short resumé of what I said last night. I will try to do it as if it were a good TV series. So, what happened in the first episode? Very few important things. I have tried to explain why I was interested in the practice of self-examination and confession. Those two practices seem to me to be good witnesses for a major problem, which is the genealogy of the modern self. This genealogy has been my obsession for years because it is one of the possible ways of getting rid of a traditional philosophy of the subject. I would like to outline this genealogy from the point of view of techniques, what I call techniques of the self. Among these techniques of the self, the most important, in modern societies, I think, is that which deals with the interpretive analysis of the subject, with the hermeneutics of the self. How was the hermeneutics of the self formed? This is the theme of the two lectures. Yesterday night I spoke about Greek and Roman techniques of the self, or at least about two of these techniques, confession and self-examination. It is a fact that we meet confession and self-examination very often in the late Hellenistic and Roman philosophies. Are they the archetypes of Christian confession and self-examination? Are they the early forms of the modern hermeneutics of the self? I have tried to show that they are quite different. Their aim is not, I think, to decipher a hidden truth in the depth of the individual. Their aim is something else. It is to give the individual the force of truth. Their aim is to constitute the self as the ideal unity of will and truth. Well, now let us turn toward Christianity as the cradle of Western hermeneutics of the self.] The theme is: how was what I would like to call the interpretive analysis of the self formed in our societies; or, how was formed the hermeneutics of the self in modern, or at least in Christian and modern, societies? In spite of the fact that we can find very early in Greek, in Hellenistic, in Latin cultures, techniques such as self-examination and confession, I think that there are very large differences between the Latin and Greek—the Classical—techniques of the self and the techniques developed in Christianity. And I'll try to show this evening that the modern hermeneutics of the self is rooted much more in those Christian techniques than in the Classical ones. The *gnothi seauton* is, I think, much less influential in our societies, in our culture, than it is supposed to be.

As everybody knows, Christianity is a confession. That means that Christianity belongs to a very special type of religion, religions which impose on those who practice them the obligation of truth. Such obligations in Christianity are numerous; for instance, a Christian has the obligation to hold as true a set of propositions which constitutes a dogma; or he has the obligation to hold certain books as a permanent source of truth; or, [at least in the Catholic branch of Christianity,] he has the obligation to accept the decisions of certain authorities in matters of truth [obligations not only to believe in certain things but also to show that one believes in them. Every Christian is obliged to manifest his faith].

But Christianity requires another form of truth obligation quite different from those I just men-

tioned. Everyone, every Christian, has the duty to
know who he is, what is happening in him. He has
to know the faults he may have committed: he has
to know the temptations to which he is exposed.
And, moreover, everyone in Christianity is obliged
to say these things to other people, to tell these
things to other people, and hence, to bear witness
against himself.

A few remarks. These two ensembles of obligations, those regarding the faith, the book, the
dogma, and the obligations regarding the self, the
soul, the heart, are linked together. A Christian is
always supposed to be supported by the light of
faith if he wants to explore himself, and, conversely, access to the truth of the faith cannot be conceived of without the purification of the soul. As
Augustine said, in a Latin formula I'm sure you'll
understand, *qui facit veritatem venit ad lucem.* That
means: *facite veritatem,* "to make truth inside oneself," and *venire ad lucem,* "to get access to the light."
Well, to make truth inside of oneself, and to get
access to the light of God, and so on, those two
processes are strongly connected in the Christian
experience. But those two relationships to truth,
you can find them equally connected, as you know,
in Buddhism, and they were also connected in all
the Gnostic movements of the first centuries. But

there, either in Buddhism or in the Gnostic movements, those two relationships to truth were connected in such a way that they were almost identified. To discover the truth inside oneself, to decipher the real nature and the authentic origin of the
soul, was considered by the Gnosticists as identical
with coming through to the light. [If the gnomic
self of the Greek philosophers, of which I spoke
yesterday evening, had to be built as an identification between the force of the truth and the form of
the will, we could say that there is a gnostic self.
This is the gnostic self that we can find described in
Thomas Evangilium or the Manichean texts. This
gnostic self has to be discovered inside the individual, but as a part, as a forgotten sparkle of the prim-
itive light.]

On the contrary, one of the main characteristics of orthodox Christianity, one of the main differences between Christianity and Buddhism, or
between Christianity and Gnosticism, one of the
main reasons for the mistrust of Christianity
toward mystics, and one of the most constant historical features of Christianity, is that those two
systems of obligation, of truth obligation — the one
concerned with access to light and the one concerned with the making of truth, the discovering of
truth inside oneself — those two systems of obliga-

tion have always maintained a relative autonomy. Even after Luther, even in Protestantism, the secrets of the soul and the mysteries of the faith, the self and the book, are not in Christianity enlightened by exactly the same type of light. They demand different methods and involve special techniques.

Well, let's put aside the long history of their complex and often conflictual relations before and after the Reformation. This evening I'd like to focus attention on the second of those two systems of obligation. I'd like to focus on the obligation imposed on every Christian to manifest the truth about himself. When one speaks of confession and self-examination in Christianity, one has in mind, of course, the sacrament of penance and the canonic confession of sins. But these are rather late innovations in Christianity. Christians of the first centuries knew completely different forms for the showing forth of the truth about themselves, and you'll find these obligations of manifesting the truth about oneself in two different institutions — in penitential rites and monastic life. And I would like first to examine the penitential rites and the obligations of truth, the truth obligations which are related, which are connected with those penitential rites. I will not, of course, go into the discussions which have taken place and which continue until now regarding the progressive development of these rites. I only would like to emphasize one fundamental fact: in the first centuries of Christianity, penance was not an act. Penance, in the first centuries of Christianity, penance is a status, which presents several characteristics. The function of this status is to avoid the definitive expulsion from the church of a Christian who has committed one or several serious sins. As penitent, this Christian is excluded from many of the ceremonies and collective rites, but he does not cease to be a Christian, and by means of this status he can obtain his reintegration. And this status is therefore a long-term affair. This status affects most aspects of his life—fasting obligations, rules about clothing, interdictions on sexual relations—and the individual is marked to such an extent by this status that even after his reconciliation, after his reintegration in the community, he will still suffer from a number of prohibitions (for instance, he will not be able to become a priest). So penance is not an act corresponding to a sin; it is a status, a general status in the existence.

Now, amongst the elements of this status, the obligation to manifest the truth is fundamental. I don't say that enunciation of sins is fundamental; I use a much more imprecise and obscure expression. I say that manifestation of the truth is necessary and is deeply connected with this status of penance. In fact, to designate the truth games or the truth obligations inherent to penitents, the Greek fathers used a word, a very specific word (and very enigmatic also); the word *exomologesis*. This word was so specific that even Latin writers, Latin fathers, often used the Greek word without even translating it.[15]

What does this term *exomologesis* mean? In a very general sense, the word refers to the recognition of an act. But more precisely, in the penitential rite, what was the *exomologesis*? Well, at the end of the penitential procedure, at the end and not at the beginning, at the end of the penitential procedure, when the moment of reintegration arrived, an episode took place which the texts regularly call *exomologesis*. Some descriptions are very early and some very late, but they are quite identical. Tertullian, for instance, at the end of the second century, describes the ceremony in the following manner. He wrote: "The penitent wears a hair shirt and ashes. He is wretchedly dressed. He is taken by the hand and led into the church. He prostrates himself before the widows and the priest. He hangs on the skirts of their garments. He kisses their knees."[16] And much later after this, in the beginning of the 5th century, Jerome described the penitence of Fabiola in the same way. Fabiola was a woman, a well-known Roman noblewoman, who had married a second time before the death of her first husband, which was something quite bad; she then was obliged to do penance. And Jerome describes thus this penance: "During the days which preceded Easter," which was the moment of the reconciliation, "during the days which preceded Easter, Fabiola was to he found among the ranks of the penitents. The bishop, the priests, and the people wept with her. Her hair disheveled, her face pale, her hands dirty, her head covered in ashes, she chastened her naked breast and the face with which she had seduced her second husband. She revealed to all her wound, and Rome, in tears, contemplated the scars on her emaciated hody."[17]

No doubt Jerome and Tertullian were liable to be rather carried away by such things; however, in Ambrose and in others one finds indications which clearly show the existence of an episode of dramatic self-revelation at the moment of reconciliation for the penitent. That was, specifically, the *exomologesis*.

But the term of *exomologesis* does not apply only to this final episode. Frequently, the word *exomolo-*

gesis is used to designate everything that the penitent does to achieve his reconciliation during the
period in which he retains the status of penitent.
The acts by which he punishes himself can't be dis-
associated from those by which he reveals himself.
The punishment of oneself and the voluntary
expression of oneself are bound together.

A correspondent of Cyprian in the middle of the
3rd century writes, for instance, that those who wish
to do penance must, I quote, "prove their suffering,
show their shame, make manifest their humility, and
exhibit their modesty."[18] And, in the *Paraenesis*,
Pacian says that the true penance is accomplished not
in a nominal fashion but finds its instruments in sack-
cloth, ashes, fasting, affliction, and the participation
of a great number of people in prayers. In a few
words, penance in the first Christian centuries is a
way of life acted out at all times out of an obligation
to show oneself. And that is, exactly, *exomologesis*.
[This form, attested to from the end of the 2nd
century, will subsist for an extremely long time in
Christianity, since one finds its after-effects in the
orders of penitents so important in the 15th and
16th century. One can see that the procedures for
showing forth the truth are multiple and complex.
Some acts of *exomologesis* take place in private but
most are addressed to the public.]

As you see, this *exomologesis* did not obey a judicial principle of correlation, of exact correlation, adjusting the punishment to the crime. *Exomologesis* obeyed a law of dramatic emphasis and of maximum theatricality. And neither did this *exomologesis* obey a truth principle of correspondence between verbal enunciation and reality. As you see, there is no description of penance in this *exomologesis*; no confession, no verbal enumeration of sins, no analysis of the sins, but somatic expressions and symbolic expressions. Fabiola did not confess her fault, telling somebody what she has done, but she put under everybody's eyes the flesh, the body, which has committed the sin. And, paradoxically, the *exomologesis* then consists of rubbing out the sin, restoring the previous purity acquired by baptism, and this by showing the sinner as he is in his reality—dirty, defiled, sullied.[19]

Tertullian has a word to translate the Greek word *exomologesis*; he said it was *publicatio sui*, the Christian had to publish himself.[20] Publish oneself, that means that he has two things to do. One has to show oneself as a sinner; that means, as somebody who, choosing the path of sin, preferred filthiness to purity, earth and dust to heaven, spiritual poverty to the treasures of faith. In a word, he has to show himself as somebody who chose spiritual death to earthly life. And it is for this reason that *exomologesis* was a kind of representation of death. It was the theatrical representation of the sinner as dead or as dying. But this *exomologesis* was also a way for the sinner to express his will to free himself from this world, to get rid of his own body, to destroy his own flesh, and get access to a new spiritual life. It is the theatrical representation of the sinner willing his own death as a sinner. It is the dramatic manifestation of the renunciation to oneself.

To justify this *exomologesis* and this renunciation to oneself in manifesting the truth about oneself, Christian fathers used several models. The well-known medical model was very often used in pagan philosophy: one has to show his wounds to the physicians if he wants to be healed. They also used the judicial model: one always appeases the court when spontaneously confessing one's faults. [The day of judgment, the Devil himself will stand up to accuse the sinner. If the sinner has already anticipated him by accusing himself, the enemy will be obliged to remain quiet.] But the most important model meant to justify the necessity of *exomologesis* is the model of martyrdom. The martyr is he who prefers to face death rather than abandoning his faith. [One shouldn't forget that the practice and the theory of penitence, to a great extent, were elaborated around the problem of the relapsed.... The relapsed abandons his faith in order to retain the life down here.] The sinner will be reinstated only if in turn he exposes himself voluntarily to a sort of martyrdom that everyone will witness, and which is penance, or penance as *exomologesis*. [In brief, penance, insofar as it is a reproduction of martyrdom, is an affirmation or change —of rupture with one's self, with one's past *metanoia*, of a rupture with the world, and with all previous life.] The function of such a demonstration therefore isn't to establish a personal identity. Rather, such a demonstration serves to provide this dramatic demonstration of what one is: the refusal of the self, the breaking off from one's self. One recalls what was the objective of Stoic technology: it was to superimpose, as I tried to explain to you last week, the subject of knowledge and the subject of the will by means of the perpetual rememorizing of the rules. The formula which is at the heart of *exomologesis* is, in contrary, *ego non sum ego*. The *exomologesis* seeks, in opposition to the Stoic techniques, to superimpose by an act of violent rupture the truth about oneself and the renunciation of oneself. In the ostentatious gestures of maceration, self-revelation in *exomologesis* is, at the same time, self-destruction.

Well, if we turn to the confession in monastic institutions, it is of course quite different from this *exomologesis*. In the Christian institutions of the first centuries another form of confession can be found, very different from this one. It is the organized confession in monastic communities. In a certain way, this confession is close to the exercise practiced in the pagan schools of philosophy. There is nothing astonishing in this, since the monastic life was considered the true form of philosophical life, and the monastery the school of philosophy. There is an obvious transfer of several technologies of the self in Christian spirituality from practices of pagan philosophy.

Regarding this continuity I'll quote only one witness, John Chrysostom, who describes an examination of conscience which has exactly the same form, the same shape, the same administrative character, as that described by Seneca in the *De Ira* and which I spoke about last week. John Chrysostom says, and you'll recognize exactly (well, nearly) the same words as in Seneca. Chrysostom writes: "It is in the morning that we must take account of our expenses, then it is in the evening, after our meal, when we have gone to bed and no one troubles us and disquiets us, that we must ask ourselves to account for our conduct to ourselves. Let us examine what is to our advantage and what is prejudicial. Let us cease spending inappropriately and try to set aside useful funds in the place of harmful expenses, prayers in lieu of indiscrete words."[21]

This is exactly the same administrative self-examination we talked about last week with Seneca. But these kinds of ancient practices were modified under the influence of two fundamental elements of Christian spirituality: the principle of obedience, and the principle of contemplation. First, the principle of obedience—we have seen that in the ancient schools of philosophy the relationship between the master and the disciple was, if I may say, instrumental and temporary. The disciple's obedience depended on the master's capacity to lead him to a happy and autonomous life. For a long series of reasons that I haven't time to discuss here, obedience has very different features in monastic life and above all, of course, in cenobite communities. Obedience in monastic institutions must bear on all the aspects of life; there is an adage, very well known in monastic literature, which says, "everything that one does not do on order of one's director, or everything that one does without his permission, constitutes a theft." Therefore, obedience is a permanent relationship, and even when the monk gets old, even when he becomes, in turn, a master, even then he has to keep the spirit of obedience as a permanent sacrifice of his own will.

Another feature distinguishes monastic discipline from the philosophical life. In monastic life the supreme good is not the mastership of oneself; the supreme good in monastic life is the contemplation of God. The obligation of the monk is continuously to turn his thoughts to that single point which is God, and his obligation is also to make sure that his heart, his soul, and the eye of his soul are pure enough to see God and to receive light from him.

Placed as it is under this principle of obedience and oriented towards the objective of contemplation, you understand that the technology of the self which develops in Christian monasticism presents peculiar characteristics. John Cassian's *Institutiones* and *Collationes* give a rather systematic and clear exposé of self-examination and of the confession as they were practiced among the Palestinian and Egyptian monks.[22] And I'll follow several of the indications you can find in those two books which were written in the beginning of the 5th century. First, about self-examination. The first point about self-examination in monastic life is that self examination in this kind of Christian exercise is much more concerned with thoughts than with actions. Since he continuously has to turn his thought towards God, you understand very well that the monk has to take in hand not the course of his actions, as the Stoic philosopher; he has to take in hand the course of his thoughts. Not only the passions which might cause the firmness of his conduct to vacillate; he has to take in hand the images which present themselves to the spirit, the thoughts which come to interfere with contemplation, the various suggestions which turn the attention of the spirit away from its object, that means, away from God. So much so that the primary material for scrutiny and for the examination of the self is an area anterior to actions, of course, anterior to the will also, even an area anterior to the desires—a much more tenacious material than the material the Stoic philosopher had to examine in himself. The monk has to examine a material which the Greek fathers (almost always pejoratively) call the *logismoi,* that is in Latin, *cogitationes,* the nearly imperceptible movements of thoughts, the permanent mobility of the soul. [This is the soul that Cassian described with two Greek words (undecipherable). It means that the soul is always moving and moving in all directions.] That's the material which the monk has to continuously examine in order to maintain the eye of his spirit always directed towards the unique point which is God. But, when the monk scrutinizes his own thoughts, what is he concerned with? Not, of course, with the relation between idea and reality. He is not concerned with this truth relation which makes an idea wrong or true. He is not interested in the relationship between his mind and the external world. What he is concerned with is the nature, the quality, the sub- stance of his thoughts.

We must, I think, pause for a moment on this important point. In order to understand what this permanent examination consists of, Cassian uses three comparisons. He first uses the comparison of the mill. Thought, says Cassian, thought is like a millstone which grinds the grains. The grains are, of course, the ideas which continuously present themselves in the mind. And in the comparison of the millstone, it is up to the miller to sort out amongst the grains those which are bad and those which can be admitted to the millstone because they are good. Cassian also uses the comparison of the officer who has the soldiers file past him and makes them pass to the right or to the left, allotting to each his task according to his capacities. And lastly, and that I think is the most important, the most interesting, Cassian says that, with respect to oneself, one must be like a moneychanger to whom one presents coins, and whose task consists in examining them, verifying their authenticity, so as to accept those which are authentic whilst rejecting those which are not. Cassian develops this comparison at length. When a moneychanger examines a coin, says Cassian, the moneychanger looks at the effigy the money bears, he considers the metal of which it is made, in order to know what it is and if it is pure. The moneychanger seeks to know the workshop from which it came, and he weighs it in his hand in order to know if it has been filed down or ill-used. In the same way, says Cassian, one must verify the quality of one's thoughts, one must know if they really bear the effigy of God; that is to say, if they really permit us to contemplate him, if their surface brilliance does not hide the impurity of a bad thought. What is their origin? Do they come from God, or from the workshop of the demon? Finally, even if they are of good quality and origin, have they not been whittled away and rusted by evil sentiments?

I think that this form of examination is at the same time new and historically important. Perhaps I have insisted a little too much with regard to the Stoics on the fact that their examination, the Stoic examination, was concerned with acts and rules. One must recognize, however, the importance of the question of truth with the Stoic, but the question was presented in terms of true or false opinions favorable to forming good or bad actions. For Cassian, the problem is not to know if there is a conformity between the idea and the order of external things; it is a question of examining the thought in itself. Does it really show its true origin, is it as pure as it seems, have not foreign elements insidiously mixed themselves with it? Altogether, the question is not "Am I wrong to think such a thing?" but "Have I not been deceived by the thought which has come to me?" Is the thought which comes to me, and independently of the truth as to the things it represents, is there not an illusion about myself on my part? For instance, the idea comes to me that fasting is a good thing. The idea is certainly true, but maybe this idea has been suggested not by God but by Satan in order to put me in competition with other monks, and then bad feelings about the other ones can be mixed to the project of fasting more than I do. So, the idea is true in regard to the external world, or in regard to the rules, but the idea is impure since from its origin it is rooted in bad sentiments. And we have to decipher our thoughts as subjective data which have to be interpreted, which have to be scrutinized, in their roots and in their origins.

It is impossible not to be struck by the similarity of this general theme and the similarity of this image of the moneychanger, and several texts of Freud about censorship. One could say that Freudian censorship is both the same thing and the reverse of Cassian's changer; both the Cassian changer and the Freudian censorship have to control the access to consciousnes — they have to let some representations in and to reject the others. But the function of Cassian's changer is to decipher what is false or illusory about what presents itself to consciousness and then to let in only what is authentic. For that purpose the Cassian moneychanger uses a specific aptitude that the Latin fathers called *discretio* [and the Greek fathers called *diacrisis*]. Compared to the Cassian changer, the Freudian censorship is both more perverse and more naive. The Freudian censor rejects what presents itself as it is, and the Freudian censorship accepts what is sufficiently disguised. Cassian's changer is a truth-operator through *discretio;* Freudian censorship is a falsehood-operator through symbolization. But I don't want to go further in such a parallel; it's only an indication, but I think that the relations between Freudian practice and Christian techniques of spirituality could be, if seriously done, a very interesting field of research. [What I would like to insist upon this evening is something else, or, at least, something indirectly related to that. There is something really important in the way Cassian poses the problem of truth about thought. First of all, thoughts (not desires, not passions, not attitudes, not acts) appear in Cassian's work and in all the spirituality it represents as a field of subjective data which have to be considered and analyzed as an object. And I think that is the first time in history that thoughts are considered as possible objects for an analysis. Second, thoughts have to be analyzed not in relation to their object, according to objective experience, or according to logical rules. They have to be suspected since they can be secretly altered, disguised in their own substance. Third, what man needs, if he does not want to be the victim of his own thoughts, is a perpetual hermeneutical interpretation, a perpetual work of hermeneutics. The function of this hermeneutics is to discover the reality hidden inside the thought. Fourth, this reality capable of hiding in my thoughts is a power, a power which is not of another nature than my soul, as is, for instance, the body. The power which hides inside my thoughts, this power is of the same nature as my thoughts and my soul. It is the Devil. It is the presence of somebody else in me. This constitution of thoughts as a field of subjective data needing an interpretive analysis in order to discover the power of the other in me, I think, if we compare it to the Stoic technologies of the self, is quite a new way of organizing the relationships between truth and subjectivity. I think that hermeneutics of the self begins there.]

But we have to go further, for the problem is, how is it possible to perform, as Cassian wishes, how is it possible to perform continuously this necessary self-examination, this necessary self-control of the tiniest movements in thoughts? How is it possible to perform this necessary hermeneutics of our own thoughts? The answer given by Cassian and his inspirators is both obvious and surprising. The answer given by Cassian is, well, you interpret your thoughts by telling them to the master or to your spiritual father. You interpret your thoughts by confessing not, of course, your acts, not confessing your faults, but by continuously confessing the movement you can notice in your thoughts. Why is this confession able to assume this hermeneutical role? One reason comes to mind: in exposing the movements of his heart, the disciple permits his *seigneur* to know those movements and, thanks to his greater experience, to his greater wisdom, the *seigneur*, the spiritual father, can better understand what's happening. His seniority permits him to distinguish between truth and illusion in the soul of the person he directs.

But such is not the principal reason that Cassian invokes to explain the necessity of confession. For Cassian, there is a specific virtue of verification in this act of verbalization. Amongst all the examples that Cassian quotes there is one which is particularly enlightening on this point. Cassian quotes the following anecdote: a young monk, Serapion, incapable of enduring the obligatory fast, every evening stole a loaf of bread. But, of course, he did not dare to confess it to his spiritual director, and one day this spiritual director, who no doubt guessed it all, gives a public sermon on the necessity of being truthful. Convinced by this sermon, the young Serapion takes out from under his robe the bread that he has stolen and shows it to everyone. Then he prostrates himself and confesses the secret of his daily meal, and then, not at the moment when he showed the bread he has stolen, but at the very moment when he confesses, verbally confesses, the secret of his daily meal, at this very moment of the confession, a light seems to tear itself away from his body and cross the room, spreading a disgusting smell of sulphur.

In this anecdote one sees that the decisive element is not that the master knows the truth. It is not even that the young monk reveals his act and restores the object of his theft. It is the confession, the verbal act of confession, which comes last and, in a certain sense, by its own mechanics, makes the truth, the reality of what has happened, appear. The verbal act of confession is the proof, is the manifestation of truth. Why? Well, I think it is because what marks the difference between good and evil thoughts, following Cassian, is that the evil ones cannot be referred to without difficulty. If one blushes in recounting them, if one seeks to hide his own thoughts, if even quite simply one hesitates to tell his thoughts, that is the proof that those thoughts are not as good as they may appear. Evil inhabits them. Thus verbalization constitutes a way of sorting out thoughts which present themselves. One can test their value according to whether they resist verbalization or not. Cassian gives the reason for this resistance: Satan as principle of evil is incompatible with the light, and he resists when confession drags him from the dark caverns of the conscience into the light of explicit discourse. I quote Cassian: "A bad thought brought into the light of day immediately loses its veneer. The terrible serpent that this confession has forced out of its subterranean lair, to throw it out into the light and make its shame a public spectacle, is quick to retreat."[23] Does that mean that it would be sufficient for the monk to tell his thoughts aloud even when alone? Of course not. The presence of somebody, even if he does not speak, even if it is a silent presence, this presence is requested for this kind of confession, because the *abbé*, or the brother, or the spiritual father, who listens to this confession is the image of God. And the verbalization of thoughts is a way of putting under the eyes of God all the ideas, images, suggestions, as they come to consciousness, and under this divine light they show necessarily what they are.

From this, we can see (1) that verbalization in itself has an interpretive function. Verbalization contains in itself a power of *discretio* [a power of *diacrisis*, of differences]. (2) This verbalization is not a kind of retrospection about past actions. The verbalization Cassian imposes on the monks, this verbalization has to be a permanent activity, as contemporaneous as possible to the stream of thoughts. (3) This verbalization must go as deep as possible in the depth of the thoughts. These, whatever they are, have an unapparent origin, obscure roots, secret parts, and the role of verbalization is to excavate these origins and those secret parts. (4) As verbalization brings to the external light the deep movement of the thought, it also leads, by the same process, the human soul from the reign of Satan to the law of God. This means that verbalization is a way for the conversion [for the rupture of the self] (for the *metanoia,* the Greek fathers said), for the conversion to develop itself and to take effect. Since the human being was attached to himself under the reign of Satan, verbalization as a movement toward God is a renunciation to Satan, and a renunciation to oneself. Verbalization is a self-sacrifice. To this permanent, exhaustive, and sacrificial verbalization of the thoughts which was obligatory for monks in the monastic institution, to this permanent verbalization of thoughts, the Greek fathers gave the name of *exagoreusis.*[24]

Thus, as you see, in the Christianity of the first centuries, the obligation to tell the truth about oneself was to take two major forms, the *exomologesis* and the *exagoreusis,* and as you see they are very different from one another.

On the one hand, the *exomologesis* is a dramatic expression by the penitent of his status of sinner, and this in a kind of public manifestation. On the other hand, the *exagoreusis,* we have an analytical and continuous verbalization of thoughts, and this

in a relation of complete obedience to the will of
the spiritual father. But it must be remarked that
this verbalization, as I just told you, is also a way
of renouncing one's self and no longer wishing to
be the subject of the will. Thus the rule of confession in *exagoreusis*, this rule of permanent verbalization, finds its parallel in the model of martyrdom which haunts *exomologesis*. The ascetic maceration exercised on the body and the rule of permanent verbalization applied to the thoughts, the
obligation to macerate the body and the obligation
of verbalizing thoughts—those things are deeply
and closely related. They are supposed to have the
same goals and the same effect. So much that one
can isolate as the common element to both practices the following principle: the revelation of the
truth about oneself cannot, in those two early
Christian experiences, the revelation of the truth
about oneself cannot be dissociated from the obligation to renounce oneself. We have to sacrifice the
self in order to discover the truth about ourselves,
and we have to discover the truth about ourselves
in order to sacrifice ourself. Truth and sacrifice,
the truth about ourselves and the sacrifice of ourselves, are deeply and closely connected. And we
have to understand this sacrifice not only as a radical change in the way of life but as the conse-

quence of a formula like this: you will become the subject of the manifestation of truth when and only when you disappear or you destroy yourself as a real body or as a real existence.

Let's stop here. I have been both too long and much too schematic. I would like you to consider what I have said only as a point of departure, one of those small origins that Nietzsche liked to discover at the beginning of great things. The great things that those monastic practices announced are numerous. I will mention, just before I finish, a few of them. First, as you see, the apparition of a new kind of self, or at least a new kind of relationship to our selves. You remember what I told you last week: the Greek technology, or the philosophical techniques, of the self tended to produce a self which could be, which should be, the permanent superposition in the form of memory of the subject of knowledge and the subject of the will. [What I call the gnomic self. In the beginning of this lecture, I indicated that Gnostic movements were intent on constituting an ontological unity, the knowledge of the soul and the knowledge of being. Then what could be called the gnostic self could be constituted in Christianity.]

I think that in Christianity we see the development of a much more complex technology of the self. This technology of the self maintains the difference between knowledge of being, knowledge of the word, knowledge of nature, and knowledge of the self, and this knowledge of the self takes shape in the constitution of thought as a field of subjective data which are to be interpreted. The role of interpreter is assumed through a continuous verbalization of the most imperceptible movements of thought—that's the reason we could say that the Christian self which is correlated to this technique is a gnosiologic self.

And the second point which seems to me important is this: you may notice in early Christianity an oscillation between the truth-technology of the self oriented toward the manifestation of the sinner, the manifestation of being—what we would call the ontological temptation of Christianity, and that is the *exomologesis*—and another truth-technology oriented toward the discursive and permanent analysis of thought—that is, the *exagoreusis,* and we could see there the epistemological temptation of Christianity. And, as you know, after a lot of conflicts and fluctuations, the second form of technology, this epistemological technology of the self, or this technology of the self oriented toward the permanent verbalization and discovery of the most imperceptible movements of our self, this form became victorious after centuries and centuries, and it is nowadays dominating.

Even in these hermeneutical techniques derived from the *exagoreusis* the production of truth could not be met, you remember, without a very strict condition: hermeneutics of the self implies the sacrifice of the self. And this is, I think, the deep contradiction, or, if you want, the great richness, of Christian technologies of the self: no truth about the self without a sacrifice of the self. [The centrality of the confession of sins in Christianity finds an explanation here. The verbalization of the confession of sins is institutionalized as a discursive truth-game, which is a sacrifice of the subject.] I think that one of the great problems of Western culture has been to find the possibility of founding the hermeneutics of the self not, as it was the case in early Christianity, on the sacrifice of the self but, on the contrary, on a positive, on the theoretical and practical, emergence of the self. That was the aim of judicial institutions, that was the aim also of medical and psychiatric practices, that was the aim of political and philosophical theory — to constitute the ground of subjectivity as the root of a positive self, what we could call the permanent anthropologism of Western thought. And I think that this anthropologism is linked to the deep desire to substitute the positive figure of man for the sacrifice which, for Christianity, was a condition for opening the self as a field of indefinite interpretation. [In addition, we can say that one of the problems of Western culture was: how could we save the hermeneutics of the self and get rid of the necessary sacrifice of the self which was linked to this hermeneutics since the beginning of Christianity.] During the last two centuries, the problem has been: what could be the positive foundation for the technologies of the self that we have been developing for centuries and centuries? But the moment, maybe, is coming for us to ask: do we really need this hermeneutics of the self [which we have inherited from the first centuries of Christianity? Do we need a positive man who serves as the foundation of this hermeneutics of the self?] Maybe the problem of the self is not to discover what it is in its positivity; maybe the problem is not to discover a positive self or the positive foundation for the self. Maybe our problem now is to discover that the self is nothing else than the historical correlation of the technology built in our history. Maybe the problem is to change those technologies [or maybe to get rid of those technologies, and then, to get rid of the sacrifice which is linked to those technologies.] And in this case, one of the main political problems nowadays would be, in the strict sense of the word, the politics of ourselves.

Well, I thank you very much.

NOTES

1 See Francois Leuret, *Du Traitement moral de la folie* (Paris: J.B. Bailliere, 1840), and Foucault, *Maladie mentale et psychologie*, 3rd ed. (Paris: PUF, 1966), 85–86; *Mental Illness and Psychology*, translated by Alan Sheridan (New York: Harper & Row, 1976), 72.

2 Edmund Husserl, *Méditations cartésiennes*, translated by Gabrielle Peiffer and Emmanuel Lewis (Paris: Arman Colin, 1931); *Cartesian Meditations: An Introduction to Phenomenology*, translated by Dorian Cairns (The Hague: Martinus Nijhoff, 1973).

3 *Les Mots et les choses* (Paris: Gallimard, 1966); *The Order of Things*, translated by Alan Sheridan, (New York: Pantheon, 1970).

4 *Naissance de la clinique* (Paris: Presses Universitaires de France, 1963, 1972); *The Birth of the Clinic*, translated by Alan Sheridan (New York: Pantheon, 1973) and *Surveiller et punir* (Paris: Gallimard, 1975); *Discipline and*

Punish, translated by Alan Sheridan (New York: Pantheon, 1977).

5 *La Volonté de savoir* (Paris: Gallimard, 1976); *The History of Sexuality, vol 1: An Introduction,* translated by Robert Hurley (New York: Pantheon, 1978); *L'Usage des plaisirs* (Paris: Gallimard, 1984); *The Use of Pleasure,* translated by Robert Hurley (New York: Pantheon, 1985); *Le Souci de soi* (Paris: Gallimard, 1984); *The Care of the Self,* translated by Robert Hurley (New York: Pantheon, 1986).

6 Jürgen Habermas, *Erkenntnis und Interesse* (Frankfurt am Main: Suhrkamp Verlag, 1968) and appendix in *Technik und Wissenschaft als "Ideologie"* (Ibid., 1968); *Knowledge and Human Interests,* translated by Jeremy Shapiro (Boston: Beacon, 1971), esp. "Appendix: Knowledge and Human Interests, A General Perspective," 313.

7 *Technologies of the Self: A Seminar with Michel Foucault,* edited by Luther H. Martin, Huck Gutman, and Patrick H. Hutton (Amherst: University of Massachusetts Press, 1988).

8 *The Foucault Effect: Studies in Governmentality,* edited by Graham Burchell et al. (Chicago: University of Chicago Press, 1991).

9 *Resumé de cours, 1970–19822* (Paris: Julliard,

1989), 133–66; "Sexuality and Solitude," *London Review of Books* 3, no. 9 (May 21–June 3, 1981): 3, 5-6.

10 Seneca, "On Anger," *Moral Essays, Volume 1,* translated hy John W. Basore, Loeb Classical Library (Cambridge, MA: Harvard University Press, *1958), 340-41.*

11 *Le Souci de soi,* 77–79; *The Care of the Self,* 60–62; "L'écriture de soi," *Corps écrit* 5 (February 1983): 21.

12 Galen, "On the Diagnosis and Cure of the Soul's Passions," in *On the Passions and Errors of the Soul,* translated by Paul W. Harkins (Ohio State University Press, 1963).

13 Plutarch, "How a Man May Become Aware of His Progress in Virtue," in *Moralia, Volume 1,* translated by Frank Cole Babbin, Loeb Classical Library (New York: Putnam, 1927), 400–57, esp. 436–57.

14 Seneca, "On Tranquility of Mind," in *Moral Essays, Volume 2,* translated by John W. Basore, Loeb Classical Library (Cambridge, MA: Harvard University Press, 1935), 202–85, esp. 202–13.

15 *Technologies of the Self,* 39–43.

16 Tertullian, "On Repentance," in *The Ante-Nicene Fathers,* edited by A. Roberts and J. Donaldson

(Grand Rapids, MI: Eerdmans, n.d., repr. 1979), 657–68, esp. " Exomologesis," chaps. 9–12, 664–66.

17 Jerome, "Letter LXXVII, to Oceanus," in *The Principal Works of St. Jerome*, translated by W. H. Freemantle, vol. 6 in A *Select Library of Nicene and Post-Nicene Fathers* (New York: Christian Literature Co., 1893), 157–62, esp. 159–60.

18 Cyprian, "Letter XXXVI, from the Priests and Deacons Abiding in Rome to Pope Cyprian ," in *Saint Cyprian: Letters (1–81)* 90–94 at 93, translated by Sister Rose Bernard Donna, C S.J., vol. 51 in *The Fathers of the Church* (Washington, DC: Catholic University of America Press, 1964).

19 Variant: "Most of the acts which constitute penance are not meant to tell the truth about the sin; their function is to show the true being of the sinner, or the true sinful being of the subject. The Tertullian expression, *publicatio sui*, is not a way of saying that the sinner has to explain his sins. The expression means that he has to produce himself as a sinner in his reality of sinner. And now the question is why the showing forth of the sinner should be capable of cancelling the sins" [Howison] .

20 "On Repentance," chap. 10.

21 See esp. St. John Chrysostom, "Homily XLII," on Matthew 12:33, in *St. Chrysostom: Homilies on the Gospel of St. Matthew*, edited by Phillip Schaff, vol. 10 in A *Select Library of the Nicene and Post-Nicene Fathers* (Grand Rapids, MI: Eerdmans, repr. 1975), 271.

22 John Cassian, *De Institutiones Coenobiorum* and *Collationes Patrum*, edited by Phillip Schaff, in vol. 11 of *A Select Library of Nicene and Post-Nicene Fathers* (Grand Rapids, MI: Eerdmans, repr. 1973).

23 John Cassian, *Second Conference of Abbot Moses*, chap. 11, 312–13 nt 312, in vol. 11 of *A Select Library of Nicene and Post-Nicene Fathers of the Christian Church*, edited by Philip Schaft and Henry Wace (Grand Rapids, MI: Eerdmans, 1955).

24 *Technologies of the Self*, 43–49.

ACKNOWLEDGEMENTS

Michel Foucault got interested in Kant very early on. He wrote his dissertation on Kant and anthropology. This preoccupation surfaces in his analysis of Kant in *The Order of Things*. But until the end of the 1960s–70s, in the various discussions he had, Foucault never referred to Kant, but to Nietzsche — the philosopher is not someone who attempts to totalize his own time, but the one who establishes a diagnosis of the present. Foucault's examination of Kant's "Was ist Aufklärung," in a sense, is the most "American" moment of Foucault's thinking, since it is in America that the necessity of tying down his own reflection to that of the Frankfurt School (Habermas, Benjamin) becomes visible. Although he doesn't explicitly refer to him in "What is Enlightenment," Foucault's discussion of "modernity" is a response to Benjamin's work on Baudelaire, which he had just discovered while teaching in Berkeley in 1983–84, as Thomas Zimmer indicated. [Ed.'s note].

Immanuel Kant's "Was ist Aufklärung?" was translated by Lewis White Beck and published in English in *Foundations of the Metaphysics of Morals* (Indianapolis, Indiana: Bobbs-Merrill Educational Publishing, 1959).

1. CRITIQUE AND ENLIGHTENMENT (Editor's title)

For the first time are gathered here together a number of lectures about Kant given by Michel Foucault on different occasions from 1978 to 1984. All refer specifically to the answer Kant gave to the question "Was ist Aufklärung?" in the German newspaper *Berlinische Monatschrifte* in 1784, exactly two hundred years before Foucualt's death.

"What is Critique" is the text of the lecture given to the French Society of Philosophy on May 27, 1978, and published in the *Bulletin de la Société française de philosophie*, t. LXXXIV, 1990. Transcript by Monique Emery, revised by Suzanne Delorme, Christian Menasseyre, François Azouvi, Jean-Marie Beyssade and Dominique Séglard. Translated by Lysa Hochroth.

"What is Revolution" [Editor's title] is the text of Foucault's first lecture at the Collège de France in 1983. This course, reviewed by the author himself, was published by Katharina von Bulow in *Le*

Magazine Littéraire in May 1987. Translated by Lysa Hochroth.

"What is Enlightenment" is the text of a French manuscript by Michel Foucault first published in English in the *Foucault Reader*, edited by Paul Rabinow (New York: Pantheon Books, 1984). Translated by Catherine Porter.

"For an Ethics of Discomfort" was first published in *Le Nouvel Observateur*, No. 754, April 23–29, 1979. It later became the Preface to Jean Daniel's *L'Ere des ruptures* (Paris: Grasset, 1979).

"What Our Present Is" is the text of an interview conducted by André Berten at the School of Criminology of the University of Louvain, Belgium, in 1981. It was first published in French in *Cahiers du GRIFFE*, No. 37–38, 1988 and translated into English by Lysa Hochroth in *Foucault Live, Collected Interviews, 1961–1984*, edited by Sylvère Lotringer (New York: Semiotext(e), 1996).

2. ABOUT THE BEGINNING
OF THE HERMENEUTICS OF THE SELF

"Subjectivity and Truth" and "Christianity and Confession" are two lectures Michel Foucault delivered in English at Dartmouth College on November 17 and 24, 1980. They were transcribed and edited by Thomas Keenan, then slightly re-edited from original tapes and footnoted by Mark Blasius. They have been further edited here to improve their fluency in English.

Foucault had given a slightly different version of this text for the Howison Lectures at Berkeley, California on October 20–21, 1980, and Paul Rabinow provided the variants added here between brackets. These two lectures were first published in *Political Theory*, Vol. 21, No. 2, May 1993, with an introduction by Mark Blasius, where additions were footnoted instead of being integrated into the text, as was done here. The general title follows a verbal suggestion Foucault himself made during his stay in Berkeley.